Ackno~~wledgement~~

M OST of the material on the women in this book came from my research for *A Guid Cause – The Women's Suffrage Movement in Scotland.* An additional source, which has appeared since I wrote that book, is volume 2 of Olive Banks: *The Biographical Dictionary of British Feminists* (Hemel Hempstead 1990). A new source for one woman was Sandra Stanley Holton's 'Silk Dresses and Lavender Kid Gloves: the wayward career of Jessie Craigen, working suffragist' in *Women's History Review*, volume 5, no 1, 1996. I learned about Dr Alice Ker from Marij van Helmond's *Votes for Women – the events on Merseyside 1870-1928* (National Museums & Galleries on Merseyside 1992). I found out much more about Elsie Inglis in the course of writing *In the Service of Life – The Story of Elsie Inglis and the Scottish Women's Hospitals* (Edinburgh 1994), and *Elsie Inglis – Founder of battlefront hospitals run entirely by women* (NMS Publishing Limited, Edinburgh 1998).

Further source material came to light on the women I researched and wrote about for the *New Dictionary of National Biography* (Annot Robinson, Helen Fraser, Fanny Parker, Ethel Moorhead, Mary Phillips, Marion Wallace-Dunlop, and Eunice Murray), including the following – Annot Robinson Collection: Manchester Central Library; Helen Moyes: *A Woman in a Man's World* (Alpha Books, Sydney 1971); Robert McAlmon: *Being Geniuses Together 1920-1930*, revised and with supplementary chapters by Kay Boyle (Doubleday, New York 1968); Newnham College Register, volume 1, 1871-1923; and Records of Students – Old Hall 1888-1909, M2, Newnham Archives.

I am very grateful for the material provided by those named below:

Helen Corr (Flora Stevenson); Elizabeth Crawford (Ethel Moorhead); David Doughan (Helen Archdale); Elizabeth Ewan (Eunice Murray);

Mary Gordon (Ethel Moorhead); Mary Henderson (Ethel Moorhead, Agnes Husband, and May Grant); Joan Huffman (Lady Frances Balfour); Pam Lunn (Priscilla Bright McLaren); Laura E Nym Mayhall (Eunice Murray); Virginia Russell (Anna Munro); and Jenni Wallace (Chrystal Macmillan).

The most important new source is Elizabeth Crawford: *The Women's Suffrage Movement – A Reference Guide 1866-1928* (London 1999), which has greatly enriched my knowledge of individual women and of the movement as a whole.

As always, Graham Sutton's editorial hand greatly improved the final text.

Leah Leneman

Illustrations page: (i) *top left, middle* and *right* (Courtesy of The Mistress and the Fellows, Girton College, Cambridge); (i) *bottom*, (v) *bottom right* (Edinburgh City Libraries); (ii) *top*, (iii) *top* and *bottom* , (iv) *top* and *bottom*, (v) *top left* and *right, bottom left* and *middle*, (vi) *top*, (vi) *bottom right*, (vii) *top left*, (viii) *top* and *bottom* (Glasgow Museums: The People's Palace), (ii) *bottom* (Trustees of the National Museums of Scotland); (vi) *bottom left* (Mitchell Library); (vii) *bottom right* (Dundee Central Library).

Cover illustrations: *front* – Anna Munro in front of a suffragette banner; *back* – Hunger strike medal; Suffragette medal reading 'Am I not a woman and a sister?'; Suffrage procession in Princes' Street, Edinburgh (all courtesy of Glasgow Museums: The People's Palace).

Contents

Introduction

THE '*Scottish Suffragettes*' – the suffragettes themselves would have appreciated this title. They understood the importance of grabbing attention, of self-promotion, of creating a public image, of hooking potential converts by brazen publicity and then, once those people were paying attention, educating them in the finer points of the cause. Thus, although the soubriquet 'suffragette' applied only to members of the militant branch of the movement, and this book is also about the non-militant 'suffragists' (including those who were active for decades before the 'suffragettes' even came on the scene), I have shamelessly used the word to try to give the book, and these women's stories, the widest possible appeal. And I have used 'Scottish' to cover any women with a substantial connection to Scotland.

For decades after World War I the depiction of the suffrage movement was almost entirely London-based. Thus the 'suffragettes' were forever chaining themselves to railings, marching, breaking windows, being arrested and forcibly fed in Holloway; always the backdrop is London.

Of course, London was important. The House of Commons was there and formed the focus of major demonstrations. Obviously, too, London had the largest population, and could draw the biggest crowds and the best press coverage. But before World War I the overwhelming dominance of the metropolis that we now take for granted was not yet in place. There was far more local democracy and far less centrality of political life, and every city and region had a thriving local newspaper that helped to shape opinion as much as, or more than, the nationals. All this was even more true of Scotland than of England. Furthermore, Henry Herbert Asquith, the Prime Minister, held a Scottish seat (East

Fife), as did several other Cabinet ministers. Scotland, therefore, was the focus of much attention. And Scottish women played their own part in the campaign for the parliamentary vote.

The point is that those women did not seek attention for themselves. Emmeline, Christabel and Sylvia Pankhurst were charismatic figures in the 'The Suffragette Movement', as Sylvia called it. They produced autobiographies that centred on their personal involvement and naturally their close acolytes were also included in the story; but the lively, articulate campaigners elsewhere in England, and in Scotland and Wales, without whom the whole thing would have gone nowhere, barely got a mention. And then there were the non-militant 'suffragists' who far outnumbered the 'suffragettes', and who are scarcely remembered *en masse*, let alone as individuals.

Some of these women were such ardent campaigners that their names appeared in countless newspaper reports, and finally, for some, on Scottish prison files. Yet they then seem to have vanished into complete obscurity. How can one reclaim the lives of such women? If it were an easy task, then this book would be the first in a series of individual lives, not a jigsaw of different lives with many key bits missing. All that can be done is to look for clues wherever they may be found and to decide that telling incomplete stories is much better than leaving them to be forgotten.

It has often been claimed that the part women played during World War I, at the battlefront and at home, was the factor that won them the vote, yet women in many other countries played just as important a role during the war years but were not given the vote when it was all over. The women who campaigned for the vote in Scotland, as elsewhere in Britain, deserve their share of the credit. And the stories of those at the forefront of the campaign, because they were strong, lively, articulate characters, cannot help but be intrinsically interesting.

Chapter 1
The Women's Suffrage Movement in Scotland

THE lives of the women in this book are of interest because they helped to win women the right to vote for their own members of parliament (MPs). The story of that campaign is the crucial background and must be summarised before those lives can be looked at.

It all began in the 1860s. At that time there was agitation for the parliamentary franchise to be extended beyond landowners to include the rising middle classes in the manufacturing cities. As in the 1832 Reform Acts, voting was to be restricted to 'male' persons, but unlike the earlier situation this restriction was not universally accepted. As part of a radical agenda for change, pressure for women's rights was growing, and when the bills for the English and Scottish Reform Acts of 1867 and 1868 were going through parliament, John Stuart Mill put forward a women's suffrage amendment. Its defeat crystallised the issue and led to the formation of women's suffrage societies in London, Manchester and Edinburgh. The Edinburgh National Society for Women's Suffrage remained active from 1867 until the vote was partially won in 1918 (when it changed its name to the National Union of Women for Equal Citizenship and continued campaigning on women's issues).

To the early suffragists there appeared no reason to doubt that collecting signatures and petitioning parliament would persuade MPs to extend the franchise to women. If they revealed the extent of the demand – which they certainly did, for between 1867 and 1876 some two million signatures were collected in Scotland – then surely men of reason would see that women should not be barred from voting for their MPs. Newspaper editorials were also sympathetic, and it seemed to be only a matter of time.

In any case, for the Victorian feminists the parliamentary franchise was only one of many rights to campaign for. In the 1860s women could not even vote in local government elections, let alone national ones. They could not obtain a higher education (and certainly not a medical education). The property laws were iniquitous for married women. All in all, there was a lot to fight for and, as we will see in the next chapter, women campaigned on all these fronts.

In January 1873 it was reported that 95 public suffrage meetings had been held in Scotland the previous year, and the chief magistrate of the town or district had usually presided. By 1874 there were local women's suffrage societies or committees in Edinburgh, Haddington, Burntisland, Dollar, Cupar, St Andrews, Perth, Dundee, Laurencekirk, Aberdeen, Dumfries, Ayr, Glasgow, Alloa, Paisley, Helensburgh, Stirling, Inveraray, Tain, Wick, Kirkwall, Stromness, Lerwick and Dingwall. Petitions to parliament came not only from unenfranchised women, but also from professional men and from town councils.

There were suffrage bills debated nearly every year, but none of them got anywhere, and in 1884 the Third Reform Act gave many more men the vote – but no women. It was clearly going to be a much harder slog than the enthusiastic women who formed the first suffrage societies had anticipated. But progress was being made on so many other fronts: higher education was opening up, married women's property acts were being passed, and women could vote in local government elections. Also crucial was the fact that both political parties, and the emerging Labour movement, began to rely on the unpaid assistance of women. The Conservatives had the Primrose League which created a Ladies' Grand Council in 1884. Members were, on the whole, content to remain in the background, but nevertheless many became interested in politics for the first time. The Scottish Women's Liberal Federation was actively feminist and suffragist.

These organisations were obviously middle class, but support was also growing amongst the working classes, for in 1892, the year after it was established, the Scottish Women's Co-operative Guild petitioned the government for the franchise to be extended to women.

By the end of the nineteenth century the 'New Woman' might be satirised, but she existed and had far wider horizons open to her than her mother or aunts. She could be a teacher or a doctor, she could own property or even her own business, in which case she would pay taxes just as a man did – but still she could not vote for her own MP. The Edinburgh society was still going strong, and in 1902 the Glasgow and West of Scotland Association for Women's Suffrage was formed. However the tactics they employed, like petitions to parliament, were those which had proved unsuccessful since 1867. What was needed was a whole new approach, and this came from an English widow, Emmeline Pankhurst, and her daughter, Christabel.

Mrs Pankhurst and Christabel formed the Women's Social and Political Union (WSPU) in Manchester in 1903. Initially it was closely linked with the emerging Labour movement. In 1905 the first act of militancy was carried out by Christabel, who interrupted a large Liberal meeting with the shout 'Votes for Women', and then spat in the eye of a policeman in order to be arrested and gain publicity. At the beginning of 1906 the United Kingdom had a new government with a large Liberal majority. The existing suffrage societies supported parliamentary candidates of any party who favoured women's enfranchisement. The WSPU initiated a new policy whereby all Liberal candidates, whatever their views on women's suffrage, were to be opposed until the Prime Minister, Henry Campbell-Bannerman, formally committed his government to support such a measure. As Scotland was a Liberal stronghold, and by-elections were frequent, it was bound to receive plenty of attention.

Heckling speakers at political meetings was considered a perfectly acceptable thing to do – by men. Heckling by women was unheard of and caused shock, anger … and publicity. Many women, who had never before even considered the matter, suddenly realised how absurd and unjust it was that they could not vote for MPs. To the older suffragists such behaviour seemed undignified and unladylike, and they dissociated themselves from it. However in Autumn 1906, when the WSPU sent Teresa Billington to Scotland to gather members and form branches, she found many ready converts. (In 1907 she married Frederick Greig and settled in Scotland; the couple adopted the name Billington-Greig.) Helen Fraser, a young woman who had never before taken an interest, was swept up into the movement and became the first WSPU organiser for Scotland. The Glasgow and West of Scotland Association refused to have any dealings with the new, militant society, but some of its most stalwart members left to join the WSPU.

In 1907 some members of the WSPU broke away to form a new society. They believed in a democratic organisation, whereas Christabel Pankhurst insisted that the WSPU was fighting a 'war' that demanded blind loyalty and obedience from its followers. The breakaway group at first called itself the National Women's Social and Political Union but later became the Women's Freedom League (WFL). Its president, Charlotte Despard, was born in Scotland in 1847, and Teresa Billington-Greig was responsible for the work in Scotland. Whether it was because so many Scottish women had been recruited by Teresa in the beginning, or because the Scots were by nature more resistant to autocracy, is unknown, but the WFL always had a very strong base in Scotland. It was smaller than the WSPU and the National Union of Women's Suffrage Societies (NUWSS), but held a balanced position as a 'militant' society that eschewed the later violence of the WSPU.

All the organisations soon had their own newspapers: the WSPU had *Votes for Women*, the WFL *The Vote*, and the NUWSS *The Common Cause*. Scottish members of the militant societies managed to get themselves imprisoned by joining in demonstrations in London. Although they were peaceful, while parliament was sitting any demonstration was illegal. NUWSS members did not take part in such demonstrations, but they did adopt new campaigning methods unheard of before the advent of the WSPU, like processions of suffrage supporters through London and Edinburgh. It is not surprising that some of the new methods should have been adopted in Scotland, for Helen Fraser, the WSPU's first Scottish organiser, defected to the NUWSS in 1908.

In 1909 the first militant demonstrations in Scotland took place in

Glasgow and in Dundee, where a group of women tried to force their way into a political meeting in the Kinnaird Hall. In England by this time a new tactic had been adopted by imprisoned suffragettes. Marion Wallace-Dunlop, a Scotswoman, went on hunger strike in protest against being treated as a criminal rather than a political prisoner in Holloway Prison and was released. Her example was followed by others, and indeed became WSPU policy, but the authorities were not about to release them all and such women were forcibly fed in Holloway, Birmingham and Newcastle. When the first women were arrested and imprisoned in Dundee, they naturally went on hunger strike, and there was great relief when they were released without suffering forcible feeding.

Whether one agreed or disagreed with militant tactics, they kept the suffrage campaign in the news, and more and more women flocked to join the cause. Societies sprang up all over Scotland, from Galashiels to Shetland. A Scottish Federation of Women's Suffrage Societies was formed under the NUWSS umbrella, with Dr Elsie Inglis as president. And a grand suffrage pageant and procession in October 1909 brought most of Edinburgh's populace out to watch the spectacle.

There was also by this time a Scottish *Anti*-Suffrage League. Women who opposed granting the vote to their own sex will find no place in this book, though it is ironic that one of them, the Marchioness of Tullibardine, later Duchess of Atholl, became one of the first women elected to parliament. Ironically, many of those who heard her speak against granting the suffrage were so impressed they could not see why on earth such a woman should *not* be allowed to vote.

The years 1910-11 were a period of truce. An all-party parliamentary committee was formed to draft a women's suffrage bill, known as the Conciliation Bill. Militancy was suspended, but all the suffrage societies continued to campaign. In 1911 the militant societies organised a census night boycott; if women were not granted full citizenship, then why should they submit to be counted?

At the end of 1911 Asquith, the Prime Minister, announced that no further time would be given to the Conciliation Bill that session. He claimed that a women's suffrage amendment would be possible to a new Reform Bill he intended to introduce to enlarge the male vote in the next session, but the WSPU considered his action a betrayal and renewed militancy. In March 1912 a three-day window-smashing raid in London resulted in over 200 arrests and imprisonments. A number of Scotswomen travelled down to take part and consequently suffered imprisonment and, in some cases, forcible feeding in Holloway. At the same time the non-militant NUWSS also changed its tactics from one of equal support for any political candidate in favour of women's suffrage to one of active support for the Labour Party, the only one with a manifesto commitment to votes for women. An 'election fighting fund' was started, and though this was opposed by many Liberal supporters, most were pragmatic enough to see the sense of it.

There was still the token promise of a women's suffrage amendment to the Reform Bill, and at the beginning of 1913 two women from Dundee and eight from Edinburgh joined a working-class deputation from all over Britain to plead the cause. However, when the debate began in parliament, the Speaker of the House dropped a bombshell: a woman's suffrage amendment to the bill would so alter its nature that it would have to be withdrawn and a new statute drawn up to be considered in a future session. The WSPU saw this as the final betrayal, and guerrilla warfare and secret arson were proclaimed by the Pankhursts as the only way forward.

At the beginning of 1913 the favoured form of militancy in Scotland was attacks on post boxes. Corrosive acid was poured into pillar boxes to destroy letters. This alienated the public more than it embarrassed the government, but the perpetrators normally escaped arrest. The scale of the attacks on property escalated, with racecourse stands, cricket pavilions, Farington Hall in Dundee, various mansions, and Leuchars railway station burnt down. Many public buildings – including Holyrood Palace – were closed for fear of attack, and security was tightened around others. There was a backlash against the suffragettes, and those who tried to speak in public found themselves facing a barrage of missiles and some very rough treatment.

The arsonists were seldom caught, but those who were faced imprisonment and a new ordeal under the so-called Cat and Mouse Act. Imprisoned suffragettes as a matter of course would immediately go on hunger (later hunger and thirst) strike. Forcible feeding caused damaging publicity for the government, so for a while prison officers did not attempt it. Under the new statute they would leave the women alone until their health was in real danger and then release them under licence, to be returned to prison as soon as their health was recovered. Suffragette prisoners did not, however, meekly return to their cells when they felt well again. Even when a watch was kept on their houses they managed to give policemen the slip and disappear. As a result, forcible feeding was resumed.

In February 1914 a suffragette was forcibly fed for the first time in Scotland. Ethel Moorhead, a particularly audacious character, had been caught at attempted fire-raising. She and her companion, Dorothea Chalmers Smith, had been imprisoned and released under the Cat and Mouse Act, but subsequently Ethel Moorhead was seen reconnoitring the grounds of Traquair House. As she was still under licence to return to prison, she was arrested and imprisoned in Calton Jail, Edinburgh. She was believed to have been involved in fire-raising during her release, so official approval was given to have her forcibly fed, starting on 21 February. This caused immense shock when word got out, for it had been believed that Scottish officials would not allow this barbarity.

On 25 February Ethel Moorhead was hurriedly released – still under licence – with double pneumonia as a result of food getting into her lungs. She was under the care of a suffragette sympathiser, Dr Grace Cadell, and the house was kept under 24 hour watch, but Ethel nevertheless escaped. The level of arson attacks was stepped up, and Whitekirk in East Lothian, one of Scotland's most beautiful medieval churches, was burnt down. In June 1914 it was decided that all suffragettes convicted in Scotland would be sent to Perth Prison where they would be forcibly fed. Dr Ferguson Watson, who had forcibly fed Ethel Moorhead, was now probationary officer at Perth.

The women in Perth Prison underwent a terrible ordeal. They were in effect in solitary confinement, apart from the periods when they were forcibly fed, in one case for as long as five weeks. Attempts were made to feed two women by the rectum, and when this was discovered there was a terrible outcry. Round the clock vigils were held outside Perth Prison, and public opinion was mobilised on the side of women.

The non-militant suffragist campaign was stalled during this final, violent period of militancy. No matter how they protested their own disapproval of attacks on property, they were bound to be tarred with the same brush. It was total impasse, for the government could not have been seen caving in to the demands of the militants, yet those militants were by then so totally committed to their cause that nothing short of war could have stopped them. As it was, on 4 August 1914, when war was declared against Germany, the WSPU announced a truce on militancy.

Although Emmeline and Christabel Pankhurst threw themselves into the war effort as fervently as they had thrown themselves into the suffrage struggle, not all women who had campaigned for the vote followed them. Within the NUWSS executive committee there was a bitter division between those who took a pro-war stance and those who were against the war, and in 1915 many of the latter resigned and went to work with organisations dedicated to peace. When the war first broke out many activists felt for the plight of wives left behind while their male breadwinners went off to fight, and both the Women's Freedom League and the Scottish Federation of the NUWSS devoted themselves to relief work at that stage. Later this was not necessary, for the war opened up many opportunities for women to work and earn a good wage.

Dr Elsie Inglis, whose medical services were curtly rejected by the War Office, suggested to the Scottish Federation and NUWSS that funds be raised to create all-women hospital units to serve Allied armies in the field, and from small beginnings the Scottish Women's Hospitals for Foreign Service grew into an amazing organisation sending out over a thousand women and raising about half a million pounds.

The WFL never gave up campaigning for the vote, and the NUWSS kept itself in readiness for the time when the franchise would be widened. It was inconceivable that working-class men who were fighting for their country would not be granted the vote, and when this happened it would be crucial to see that women were also included. There was by this time a coalition government, so the party-political fear of giving in to women's demands was no longer in operation, and all the praise being heaped on women for their work in the war effort made it possible to graciously grant them the parliamentary franchise without having to admit any dread of a new surge of suffrage militancy after the war. However, fears of being 'swamped' by a female electorate were still so great that the right was restricted to the over-30s, thereby denying it to a large proportion of the women whose war work was receiving such praise. Surprisingly, since the idea of women MPs seemed such a distant goal that it was never overtly campaigned for, the new statute (passed on 6 February 1918) also gave women the right to stand for parliament. In 1928, by which time it was clear that women voters did not upset the system in any way, the franchise was extended to the under-30s.

Some of the keenest suffragettes ceased to be politically active once the vote was won, but others continued to work within feminist organisations for, after all, the vote was not meant to be an ending but a beginning.

*   *   *

The structure of any 'group biography' is problematic. Alphabetical entries separate individuals from their context. Chronological ones involve a choice of date of birth or death, which may be unknown or irrelevant. The choice made here – to begin chronologically with the Victorian movement and then place individuals within the three main suffrage organisations – involves some arbitrary decisions. Some of the women active in the nineteenth century played an important role in the Edwardian movement and could as easily appear in either of the next two chapters. A number of women (as will be seen) transferred their allegiance at some stage from one society to another. However, those women eventually found a grouping in which they felt at home, and that is where they have been placed.

The divisions continued long after the vote had been won. Those who had belonged to the WSPU formed the Suffragette Fellowship, with a spell in prison being almost a prerequisite for membership. Their papers ended up in the Museum of London, while all the records of the NUWSS – whose members had been 'suffragists', not 'suffragettes' – went to the Fawcett Library. The WFL kept its own organisation intact until the 1960s. So, however arbitrary, placing suffragists and suffragettes within the organisation where they ultimately felt they belonged has seemed the most logical way of presenting their lives.

There were, of course, networks and connections between many of the women, and these are brought out whenever possible. However, Chapters 2 to 5 present discrete lives of individuals. Chapter 6 is different, because the small group of suffragettes who dared and risked everything at the end became so closely linked that the story of their exploits must be told as a whole, and as an exciting climax to *The Scottish Suffragettes*.

Chapter 2
The Victorians

S UFFRAGISTS in the mid-nineteenth century faced formidable obstacles. According to the prevailing ideology, women's sphere was in the home (never mind the reality that many had to work to survive), and the ideal of working-class as much as middle-class men was to be the breadwinner of the family. Pseudo-science claimed that women's brains were smaller, their bodies weaker (no matter that they bore child after child), their capacities limited. They were not permitted to go on to any further education, nor to consider any profession. They could not even vote for, let alone serve on, local government bodies, and politics were meant to be far beyond their understanding. So what hope did they have of being allowed to vote for their representatives in parliament? That was man's business. If they tried to assert themselves, then they were sneered at as 'masculine'. Such Victorian prejudices had to be overturned before the franchise could be won. Individual women of great ability were determined to do so.

Amongst the most successful were the Stevenson sisters, Flora and Louisa. They were members of a family of eleven, six of whom were girls, daughters of successful Glasgow businessman James Stevenson and his wife Jane Stewart Shannon. Two of the daughters married and, as we shall see in Chapter 4, the feminist tradition was continued into the next generation. James, a managing partner of the Jarrow Chemical Works, retired from business in 1854 when the family moved to Edinburgh to take up residence at 13 Randolph Crescent.

Louisa Stevenson was born in 1835, and Flora in 1839. After their father's death in 1866 they maintained their own household, along with two other unmarried sisters, and this became one of the centres of women's rights campaigning in Edinburgh. They were founder members of the Edinburgh Ladies Educational Association (later called the Edinburgh Association for the Higher Education of Women) in 1867 and were among 265 women who enrolled for the first courses in 1868. There was no hope at that stage of gaining admission to the universities, but the classes were taught by distinguished academics at university level, with a high standard of examination, so that though they did not lead to formal qualifications they did provide the education. And they also demonstrated women's scholarly abilities.

Naturally the sisters became involved in the suffrage campaign when it began in 1867. The year 1870 saw the creation of school boards in Britain, and women were allowed to stand as candidates, their first chance to play a part in local government. Flora was one of two women elected to Edinburgh School Board in 1873 and was so successful that she was re-elected for 33 years until her death in 1905. In 1899 she became the first woman chairman of the Board and was also elected one of the Board's representatives on the Edinburgh Educational Trust and on the Heriot Trust. Her knowledge and advice were sought by various commissions and committees. In that same year the Board paid her a personal tribute by naming a new primary school at Comely Bank after her. Her contribution to education was considered so outstanding that in 1892 she was made an Honorary Fellow of the Educational Institute of Scotland.

Further honours followed. In 1903 she was awarded an honorary degree of LLD by Edinburgh University. In January 1904 she was admitted a burgess and guild brother (*sic*) of the City of Edinburgh, when she pointed out the extent to which women, since they were first allowed onto a local government body in 1870, had proved their worth in such work. With (apparently) no personal letters surviving, it is impossible to get any real inkling of Flora Stevenson's personality, but that she was a woman of formidable powers is more than obvious.

While Flora was involved in education generally, her sister Louisa campaigned specifically for women to be allowed medical training and to qualify as doctors. The campaign was eventually successful, for from 1885 women could qualify along with men for the new Licentiate of the Royal College of Physicians and Surgeons of Edinburgh and the Faculty of Physicians and Surgeons of Glasgow. The difficulty was for women to gain the necessary training, knowledge and experience since many lecturers still barred women from their classes. Sophia Jex-Blake, who 17 years earlier had led women's first attempts in Edinburgh to receive a medical education, started her own school, enlisting sympathetic doctors to lecture and guaranteeing their fees. In 1876 Louisa Stevenson had joined forces with Sophia and another woman to buy a property in Surgeons Square, and this became the premises for the new school. Later Louisa was on the Board of the Managers of Edinburgh Royal Infirmary and was re-elected six times.

However, Louisa did not confine her interests to medicine. Along with Flora she was one of the founders of the Edinburgh School of Cookery and Domestic Economy – which was seen at the time as a great innovation and forward step for women – and became its treasurer. She was one of the first two women to be elected a member of the Parochial Board in Edinburgh. She was more active (formally) than her sister in the suffrage campaign, as a member of the executive committee of the National Union of Women's Suffrage Societies (NUWSS) in the 1890s, and representing the Edinburgh society on the parliamentary committee to handle suffrage activities among MPs. Edinburgh University conferred the honorary degree of LLD on her in 1906, two years before her death.

*   *   *

The second Edinburgh household that formed a locus for feminist campaigning was not an all-female one. Duncan McLaren was involved in the anti-slavery movement and other reforming campaigns and was known as 'the living voice of Scottish middle-class dissenting radicalism'. The daughter of his second marriage, Agnes, was at the forefront of the drive to open up medical education to women, and she herself eventually qualified as a doctor. Agnes McLaren became joint secretary of the Edinburgh National Society for Women's Suffrage when it was formed in 1867, and she remained active in the suffrage movement until her death in 1913. Meanwhile, in 1848, when he was again a widower, Duncan married a kindred spirit in Priscilla Bright, a marriage that lasted until his death 38 years later.

Priscilla was born in Rochdale, Lancashire, in 1815, the fifth of eleven children. Her father owned a weaving mill, and after receiving a good Quaker education the sisters ran a school for the mill girls, teaching them reading, writing and sewing. In common with many other Quaker families in the north of England, the Brights were active in progressive causes like the anti-slavery movement and the anti-corn law campaign, of which Priscilla's brother, John, became a leading member. She grew up living and breathing radical politics, and as the Quakers did not accept the Victorian myth of female intellectual frailty she was drawn into such causes herself. So actively political was this family that in 1886 she had a husband, two sons, two brothers and a nephew all sitting as MPs in the House of Commons; subsequently a grandson was also elected. One of her brothers, Jacob, was at the forefront of women's claims in the House of Commons. She, of course, was debarred from even voting.

Duncan McLaren was a close friend and political associate of her brother, John, and was 15 years older than Priscilla. They first met in 1842 and married in the registry office at Rochdale in 1848, whereupon the Quakers disowned her for 'marrying out'. Thereafter Priscilla's home and political life was in Edinburgh. Duncan was Lord Provost of Edinburgh from 1851 to 1854 and Liberal MP from 1865 to 1881. In January 1870 he presided over the first public meeting to be held in Edinburgh in favour of women's suffrage, and in 1881 he introduced and carried the first Married Women's Property (Scotland) Act. If Priscilla could not participate formally, she could still play an active part in the important feminist campaigns. Unintimidated by public speaking, Priscilla was the obvious choice as first president of the Edinburgh National Society for Women's Suffrage in 1867.

In 1882 Scottish women were granted the municipal franchise and challenged the illogicality of being considered capable of voting for their councillors but not for their members of parliament. During that year the annual British demonstration in favour of women's suffrage was held for the first time in a Scottish city, at the St Andrew's Hall, Glasgow. The hall was packed with women (only a handful of men were admitted), and Priscilla McLaren addressed the meeting: 'Scotland has witnessed many a noble gathering in the cause of liberty, but never one nobler than the one I look upon tonight, over which I have the honour to preside.'

(Her obituarist in *The Times* would later comment that she was 'an excellent speaker – singularly free from egotism'.)

The failure of the Second Reform Act in 1884 to admit any women voters was a setback, but the campaigning continued. At the annual meeting of the Edinburgh National Society in October 1893, Priscilla – still going strong as president at the age of 78 – commented on the way women were now able to sit on school and parochial boards and to take part in many forms of public work which had been denied them earlier in the century. Many ladies had told her 'what suffering invalid lives they led until they engaged in public questions'.

Priscilla McLaren was active in the women's movement throughout her long life. Toward the end of it, in 1901, when in north-west England factory women were being mobilised to demand the vote, she was delighted and raised money for the 'Factory Women's Movement'. Two days before her death in 1906, at the age of 91, after the first suffragettes had been arrested and imprisoned, Priscilla dictated a letter of 'sympathy and admiration' for their 'noble courage and self-sacrifice' to the nine women in Holloway Prison.

*   *   *

The third household was that of Sarah Elizabeth Siddons Mair and her mother. Sarah was only 19 when she started the Edinburgh Essay Society in 1865 (from 1869 the Ladies Edinburgh Debating Society). She lived an active life to the age of 95 in 1941, so to put her in the chapter on 'Victorians' may seem odd, but her contribution to the early women's movement was so striking that she simply has to be placed here. The importance of the debating society was that for the first time it offered women a forum to discuss public affairs without fear of male scorn. The chance to express and contest their views amongst a group of other intelligent women gave them a schooling in public speaking and the confidence to embark on campaigning.

From her earliest years Sarah, a great-granddaughter of the actress Sarah Siddons, was described as 'an accomplished and eloquent speaker, gifted beyond the ordinary with a musical voice ... perfect self-possession and poise of manner and address, both on the public platform and in private'. When her father lost a fortune on railway shares her mother had supplemented the family income by giving readings of Shakespeare. 'We were literally fed and clothed on Shakespeare,' Sarah later remembered.

Out of the Debating Society came, amongst other things, the Edinburgh Association for the University Education of Women, which persuaded Professor Masson and others to set up university-standard classes for women, which by their success helped to ensure the eventual admission of women to a full university degree. Sarah became one of the founders of St George's School for Girls, and of Masson Hall, the first university hall of residence for women. She was also involved in the Edinburgh women's hospitals set up by Sophia Jex-Blake and Elsie Inglis. She was the natural successor to Priscilla McLaren as president of the Edinburgh National Society for Women's Suffrage, and when the Scottish Federation was formed in 1909 she became president of that as well. The NUWSS paper, the *Common Cause*, commented that her 'generous enthusiasm for the enfranchisement of women, her genial presence and racy speech have done much to make our cause popular in Edinburgh'. When war broke out and a new organisation – the Scottish Women's Hospitals for Foreign Service – was born out of the Scottish Federation, Sarah served as president of the Hospitals Committee throughout.

Sarah was awarded an honorary degree of LLD by Edinburgh University in 1920 and a DBE in 1931 for her work in the cause of women's education. She never married, and her home in Chester Street remained a centre for the women's movement; she kept the Debating Society going there until her 90th year, in 1935.

* * *

In striking contrast to a woman whose antecedents and later life are so well documented is the case of Jane Taylour, who appeared like a meteor on the Scottish scene only to vanish within three short years. By 1870 there were branches of the National Society for Women's Suffrage in Aberdeen, Glasgow, St Andrews and Galloway. The honorary secretary of the Galloway one was Jane Taylour of Belmont, Stranraer. Miss Taylour was a good public speaker and was undaunted by travel. By April 1871 Priscilla McLaren was able to tell a women's suffrage conference in London that Miss Taylour had not only arranged seven meetings herself, she had also addressed no fewer than 41 public meetings on the subject. All of them had been presided over by chief magistrates of burghs, sheriffs of counties, church ministers and other influential men, resulting in petitions being sent to parliament in favour of women's suffrage. Priscilla made it clear that Jane Taylour received no payment for this work, so she clearly had independent means – and no male family members to restrict her activities.

Her persona was an important part of her appeal. The caricature of the suffragist was of a strident battleaxe, but of Jane (in connection with a lecture at Wigtown) it was said that 'her composition is chaste and elegant, her voice distinct and agreeable, and her manner attractive and graceful'.

In autumn 1871 Jane travelled further afield (often accompanied by Agnes McLaren), speaking at Inveraray, Oban, Inverness, Thurso, Wick, Tain, Dingwall, Forres and Elgin, and at Kirkwall and Stromness in Orkney. At the Kirkwall meeting the chairman, Provost Bain, admitted at the outset that he did not believe women should be enfranchised since he believed that parliament would always look after their interests.

But when he closed the meeting, by praising the 'tact, eloquence, and singularly lucid manner in which she has advanced the claims of her sex', he confessed that his 'former opinions on the subject which she has so well treated, have been considerably shaken'. Much of this would have been due to the lack of threat in both her persona and words. She discussed some of the unjust laws 'that press so barbarously upon those women who have had the misfortune to unite themselves to wicked and unprincipled men', but she insisted that women did not want to set themselves up in competition with men:

> *We do not want to usurp anything, or to do anything unseemly or out of order, but to do our proper part in helping on the world's reform – helping on with a woman's power, and in a woman's way, all that is wise, elevating, humane, and holy.*

Jane Taylour continued to travel and lecture during the next two years, and in summer 1873 she was presented with a testimonial consisting of a piece of jewellery and 150 guineas for her work. By that time she had delivered 152 lectures in Scotland, but at the end of that year she left for England. She apparently remained active in the suffrage movement, for her name appears as a member of the executive committee of one of the main suffrage societies in England in the 1880s and '90s, and she was still alive in 1901 when she was a vice-president of the NUWSS, but beyond that nothing more is known of her life.

* * *

Jane Taylour was not the only Victorian woman to venture as far afield as Orkney and Shetland, for Jessie Craigen also did so early in the 1870s. She was a very different character. Born in 1834 or 1835, she was 'the restless daughter of a Highland seafaring father and an Italian actress mother', who began life as an actress herself but then felt 'religious scruples' and abandoned the theatre to speak first for the temperance movement and then the suffrage movement. Initially she was not employed by the movement but simply collected minimum expenses to keep her going, often speaking outdoors to working-class audiences. Whether speaking to such crowds, or to the more genteel gatherings of the suffrage societies, she was an electrifying orator who swept her hearers up with her passion. But she was not ladylike (in fact her appearance was sometimes described as 'outlandish'), and attempts by her mentors in the movement to mould her into their image did not succeed. One newspaper report (written by someone with a sense of humour) praised her speech and went on:

> *... although at times she was rather short of breath, and the perspiration stood in beads upon her massive features, the sound of her deep tones reverberating through the hall must have made the men outside believe that something awful was happening to the wives and sweethearts whom they waited for so patiently.*

By this time Jessie was employed by the suffrage movement, but she was also involved in setting up a woman's union among Dundee's jute workers and, with support from the Aberdeen Trades Council, a women's union in Aberdeen. She spent more time in England than Scotland, but naturally stressed her Scottish origins when speaking to audiences north of the border. Unfortunately, though she was an eloquent and committed speaker, she was also erratic and undisciplined and perfectly capable of going off on a complete tangent from the subject she was meant to be speaking on. She died in 1899, aged 64, by which time she had alienated virtually all of her former supporters. But she was a colourful character and a formidable woman, who deserves to be remembered.

Chapter 3
The National Union of Women's Suffrage Societies

LOUISA Innes Lumsden was born in 1840 and died, aged 95, in 1935, thus spanning the two centuries. She was born in Aberdeen, the seventh and youngest child of Clements Lumsden and his wife Jane Forbes. Her father, an advocate, died when she was twelve and she went to live in Cheltenham. She received some education there, then in Belgium, and eventually at a finishing school in London, but her intellect and strong personality made the conventionally-restricted life of a middle-class Victorian young woman hard to stomach. When university-standard lectures were set up in Edinburgh in 1868, Louisa was allowed to return to Scotland to take part.

Soon after this Emily Davies in England was founding a new college for women, later to become Girton, Cambridge, and she recruited Louisa as one of her students. Louisa became one of the first women to take the Cambridge honours examination, achieving honours in the Classical Tripos in 1873. She remained at Girton as a classics tutor for some time, but was unhappy and went on to Cheltenham Ladies College as a classics teacher. Apparently she was not happy there either and was therefore delighted when the Ladies Educational Council of St Andrews asked her to take charge of a new girls' school they planned to set up.

It was as headmistress of St Leonard's School (from 1877) that Louisa became best known. The school was organised rather like a conventional boys school, with stress placed on physical development and a team spirit in games, and a high level of academic input, with mathematics and classics forming part of the curriculum. She remained as headmistress for five years, and the school was successful, however in common with other women with strong personalities she fell out with different members of staff at various times and never settled down in her role. There were also difficulties of a more personal nature with an ex-Girton woman, Constance Maynard, who came with her to Scotland, and with whom she had a 'stormy love affair' which did not work out.

After leaving St Leonard's in 1882 she settled in Aberdeen and was an active member of two school boards. In 1895 she returned to St Andrews as warden of a new university hall of residence for women students. She had great ambitions for this, but once again personality clashes – with the governing committee this time – led to her resignation in 1900.

It goes without saying that Louisa Lumsden was always in favour of votes for women, but until the suffrage campaign was revived in the early twentieth century her priority was women's education. Aberdeen was never a major centre for suffrage campaigning, but in 1908, when the movement was taking off, the Aberdeen Suffrage Association asked her to become its president: 'I agreed, only stipulating that I should not require to give up much time to it; but I soon found that little time was left for anything else.'

Louisa made an unusual contribution to the campaign at an early stage, for she had a horse-drawn caravan which she offered to activists like Helen Fraser for campaign tours. A convinced constitutionalist, she never condoned militancy yet expressed the ambivalence felt by many of that faction: 'One has a *mean* feeling when one is quietly enjoying the good things of life & others are in prison for their convictions!'

In spite of her English schooling, Louisa was resolutely Scottish. In response to an appeal for funds from the NUWSS she wrote that she would give what she could afford and would 'send it joyfully did I not wholly object to be addressed as a woman "of England"! That puts my back up thoroughly!' She was also an active speaker. With Lady Frances Balfour she addressed meetings at Alloa and Stirling, with Dr Elsie Inglis at Inverness and Banff, and so on. Of a meeting in Edinburgh in 1910, the *Common Cause* reported that she spoke as always 'with originality and fervour'.

In summer 1913, at the end of a suffrage 'pilgrimage' from all parts of the country, Louisa addressed the crowd from one of two platforms in Hyde Park occupied by the Scottish Federation: 'People came up to congratulate me, one man saying he came from Perth, another from Aberdeen and so on. Scotsmen all, except one Englishman, who said he came from Hampstead, but *must* shake hands with me.' In March 1914 she was elected onto the Scottish Federation executive committee, and in May of that year she moved from Aberdeen to Edinburgh, receiving fulsome praise from both the Aberdeen newspapers for all her contributions to that city.

Louisa harboured no doubts about the justness of the World War I and helped to recruit for the Seaforth Highlanders. Afterwards she wrote that 'of all the changes brought in that "tremendous time" one alone was welcome and needs no regret: the new opportunities offered to women to serve their country and to prove that they were worthy of citizenship'.

During the 1920s she worked for the Unionist Party and Women's Rural Industries. Louisa Lumsden represents an important strand of the feminism that spanned the nineteenth and twentieth centuries.

*   *   *

Dr Elsie Inglis was another Victorian feminist whose greatest involvement in the suffrage movement was during the Edwardian era, though she did not live quite long enough to be able to vote herself.

Elsie was born in India during the heyday of the British Empire, in August 1864. She had a happy childhood, with a particularly close bond to her father John, a magistrate and senior civil servant. She remained devoted to her sisters and their children in later life. John Inglis was not in accord with the tougher imperialist line being imposed on India in the later nineteenth century, so he retired young and in 1878 the family settled in Edinburgh. Elsie's dream was of a medical career, but after her mother's death in January 1885 she did not feel that she could leave her father. Fortuitously in 1886 Sophia

Jex-Blake started the Edinburgh School of Medicine for Women, which meant that Elsie could continue to live at home while pursuing her career, a goal with which her father was entirely in sympathy.

Sophia Jex-Blake's abrasive personality had antagonised many in her earlier struggles for women's right to a medical education, and her dictatorial temperament was not well suited to running a school for the kind of independent, strong-minded women seeking to become doctors. Inevitably a row broke out, insults turned to litigation, and Elsie sided with the rebels. While the court case was pending, Elsie began to organise an alternative medical education. With the help of her father and his influential friends she created the New Medical College for Women, which soon became a viable concern. Elsie also studied in Glasgow and Dublin, and spent some time as resident medical officer at the New Hospital for Women in London.

John Inglis' death in 1894 shattered Elsie; no other man came close to matching him in her eyes. She threw herself into her medical career, going into partnership with Dr Jessie MacGregor in Edinburgh, and eventually starting her own small hospital, the Hospice. Subsequently she also headed the Bruntsfield Hospital, founded by Dr Jex-Blake.

But Elsie also had another outlet for her energies and for her grief. She became aware at an early stage in her medical career of the tyranny exercised by husbands over their wives, and her period at the New Hospital for Women strongly reinforced her feminism. (Elizabeth Garrett Anderson, founder of the hospital, had been involved in the early days of the suffrage campaign; and her sister, Millicent Garrett Fawcett, was president of the NUWSS.) In fact, during that period Elsie found herself making her first suffrage speech. When she returned to Edinburgh she became honorary secretary of the executive committee of the Edinburgh National Society for Women's Suffrage. While her medical career absorbed most of her time during the 1980s, her involvement in the suffrage campaign gave her life an added dimension.

Then in 1905 the whole movement was galvanised. The 'suffragists', who, like Elsie, did not agree with militancy, found themselves caught up in a campaign that was suddenly forcing its way onto the pages of every newspaper in the country. In her role of secretary of the Edinburgh society she became involved in organising and supervising speakers, demonstrations, processions. She herself travelled around Scotland as a speaker, presenting incidents from her medical experience to illustrate the injustices she daily witnessed, such as husbands refusing consent to life-saving operations for their wives, or insisting on having them released from hospital so that they could go back to looking after the house. When the Scottish Federation of Women's Suffrage Societies was formed under the NUWSS umbrella in 1909, Elsie became honorary secretary of that as well. Her friend, Lady Frances Balfour, later wrote that after the explosion of suffrage activity Elsie, while making sure that her patients did not suffer, nevertheless 'sacrificed her professional prospects in a large measure for her work for the franchise'.

When World War I broke out in August 1914 Elsie was 50 and unwell, but the need for medical assistance seemed to her so urgent that she immediately offered her services to the War Office, only to be rebuffed with the words: 'My good lady, go home and sit still.' Instead she suggested to the Scottish Federation the idea of offering all-women medical units to allied governments. Such units would provide women doctors, as well as nurses, orderlies, administrators and drivers to tend allied casualties. They would prove that medical women's work did not have to be restricted to obstetrics and gynaecology. And they would demonstrate women's fitness for the vote. The Serb and French governments accepted the offer, money began to pour in, and the Scottish Women's Hospitals for Foreign Service (SWH) was born.

By the end of the war half a million pounds had been raised by the SWH, and over a thousand women had gone out to the battle zones, mainly in Serbia, France, and Macedonia. (From the British authorities came nothing but obstruction.) Elsie was chief medical officer of one of the first units in Serbia and was for some time a prisoner of war when the country was invaded. After her return she had a dramatic quarrel with the Hospitals Committee – she did not always find it easy to work in tandem with others whose vision, she felt, was more plodding and restricted – after which she returned to serve in the field, with the Serb forces in Russia and Romania. It was a difficult period, with the mobile hospital unit having to retreat from the enemy on three separate occasions, and what no one but her sisters knew was that she was suffering from cancer. She made it back to Britain in November 1917 – having evacuated her team across thousands of miles – and died the following day.

Elsie was a heroine, and her death caused national shock and grief. Her body lay in state in St Giles' Cathedral; Queen Mary sent a message of condolence to her sister; her funeral in Edinburgh was followed by a memorial service in Westminster where members of parliament, government ministers, British diplomats, heads of Red Cross and Army Medical Services, representatives of French, Italian and Russian embassies and Serbian, Belgian, and Romanian legations, lords, ladies, suffragists, army and navy officers, and many other distinguished people paid homage to her. The anti-suffrage argument that women could not be equal citizens because they could play no part in a war was well and truly refuted by Elsie Inglis and the SWH.

*   *   *

One of those who told Elsie's story to the world was her old friend and fellow suffrage campaigner, Lady Frances Balfour. There was little sympathy for the cause within aristocratic circles; upper-class women with money and position who wanted power were able to wield it, while many were apolitical if not actively opposed to women's suffrage. But to Frances Balfour the male monopoly of politics was unacceptable.

Born as Lady Frances Campbell in 1858, she was the fifth daughter and tenth of twelve children of the Duke and Duchess of Argyll. Her childhood was spent between Inveraray Castle, Roseneath Castle in Dunbartonshire, and Argyll Lodge in London. She had a congenital hip dislocation which meant her right leg was shorter than the left, necessitating a built-up shoe, and she later attributed her fiery temper to the years of physical immobility forced on her as a child because of her disability. Her grandmother, the Duchess of Sutherland, and her own mother were active in the anti-slavery movement, and she grew up in an intensely political Whig environment, where current issues were discussed by the men and women of the family round the dinner table.

There was initial opposition to her suitor, Eustace Balfour, since he came from a Tory family – indeed, his elder brother, Arthur Balfour, later became Conservative Prime Minister – but this was overcome, and they were married in 1879. Initially they shared an interest in art and architecture, but from about 1882 Eustace became obsessed with the idea of a volunteer army and was involved in military circles, spending long periods of time on the Continent away from his family. The couple had five children, and though they ended up with little in common (Eustace, an alcoholic, did not believe in women's suffrage), Frances always maintained absolute loyalty to him. But her life was lived separately, on her terms.

In spite of having married into a Tory family, Frances remained Liberal in her outlook, and it was her work with the Women's Liberal Unionist Association that brought her into the suffrage movement in the late 1880s. For the next quarter of a century it was central to her life, and she became a leader of the constitutional suffragists, serving on the executive committee of the NUWSS from its formation in 1897. She was active in marching, writing, and speaking on the subject throughout Scotland and England. (Between 1910 and 1912 she averaged three speeches a week to suffragist meetings from Inverness to Plymouth.) At the same time she worked behind the scenes, trying to use her family connections to raise support among MPs.

When the Women's Social and Political Union (WSPU) raised the profile of the women's suffrage movement, Frances formed part of a suffragist deputation to the Prime Minister, Asquith, in London at the beginning of 1908. She wrote about its 'comic side' to one of her sons: Asquith's secretary had demanded an assurance that no violence would be used. 'Our oldest member Miss [Emily] Davies, over 80, was with us, and we told her this was aimed at her.' But in fact at that very moment members of the WSPU were demonstrating outside the Houses of Parliament, and since any demonstration was illegal while Parliament was sitting, those women were arrested. Frances wrote to her son: 'I don't know whether I like the policy, but I do admire the courage and resource of the women.'

Numerically the main beneficiaries of the publicity raised by the militants were the constitutional societies; in 1910, after Frances addressed three 'drawing room' meetings organised by the Glasgow and West of Scotland Association for Women's Suffrage, 100 new members were signed up. Other peripheral societies were also formed. When the Scottish Churches' League for Women's Suffrage was established in 1912, Frances, already devoted to the Church of Scotland (she was one of the few women regularly to attend the annual General Assembly), became its president.

The rise in militant violence after 1912 was difficult for suffragists, but Frances always saw both sides. After Emily Wilding Davison threw herself in front of King George V's horse at the Derby, Frances admired 'the courage that can face a cataract of galloping horses, and meet with a violent and painful death'. She did not agree with the militants, but, she wrote to her son, 'I think they teach us the old story that what people will die for has behind it ultimate success'. The burning down of Whitekirk church in 1914 by suffragettes caused her great anguish, and she helped to organise a fund for the restoration of the church ('as suffragists'). Nevertheless, she also wrote a letter to *The Scotsman* to argue that the cause of women's suffrage was no less just because of the criminal acts of some of its supporters.

Frances always campaigned for women's rights on a variety of fronts, and she was one of only two women appointed to the Royal Commission on Divorce and Matrimonial Causes which sat from 1910 to 1912. She was granted an honorary degree of DLitt by the University of Durham in 1919 and LLD by Edinburgh University in 1921. Her stance during World War I, like that of the NUWSS president and some of the other executive committee members, was that the military conflict was necessary. She was very active in the London

Committee for the Scottish Women's Hospitals. After the vote was won she continued working for women's rights through the National Council of Women of Great Britain and Ireland, becoming a member of the executive committee in 1917, president in 1921, and serving as a vice-president until her death.

Lady Frances Balfour wrote several books, including a biography of Dr Elsie Inglis, and her own autobiography, *Ne Obliviscarsis – Dinna Forget*. Notorious for wielding 'the dagger of sarcastic wit with the same zest as her ancestors had wielded the broadsword', she believed in absolute equality for men and women, but had no sympathy with the notion of a 'sex war'. She died in February 1931 of pneumonia and heart failure.

*   *   *

The women so far discussed in this chapter joined the suffrage movement in the nineteenth century, before the advent of militancy. Helen Fraser was typical of the younger generation in not having given a thought to women's rights until the Women's Social and Political Union (WSPU) burst upon the scene.

Born in 1881, one of her earliest memories was 'as a very small child, being clutched by my mother as I almost fell out of a high window to look down on Queen Victoria'. Her parents were born in Caithness, but her father went to Edinburgh as a tailor's cutter, then to Leeds (where Helen was born), and finally to Glasgow, where the family settled, and he established a wholesale clothing firm. Helen was one of a family of ten (though two died in childhood), which she described as having 'wide interests and with that Scot's weakness for argument, quite capable of ending up in quarrels, but we had one virtue – nobody was allowed to carry a feud to the next meal or overnight'. Her father, who was a member of Glasgow City Council for years, strongly believed in improving conditions for workers.

In her twenties Helen's life was that of a typical middle-class young woman, going to balls and dances, playing tennis, putting on amateur theatricals, collecting for charity, and visiting families in the poorer districts of the city. But from the day she first heard Teresa Billington-Greig 'expounding logically, factually, forcefully with telling illustrations, of the need for women to vote', all this changed. Having been inspired by that leading member of the WSPU she joined that organisation, trying to persuade the staid Glasgow and West of Scotland Association for Women's Suffrage of the validity of militant tactics, and instigating a Scottish WSPU.

When Teresa Billington-Greig and others broke with the Pankhursts and formed the Women's Freedom League in 1907, Helen did not follow. But 1908, when the first stones were thrown, and the Pankhursts approved, Helen resigned from the WSPU. 'You don't use violence, you use *reason* to get the vote,' she told Mrs Pankhurst. It was a major rift for, as she herself realised, many Scottish WSPU members 'regard me as the movement', and indeed there was no longer a separate Scottish WSPU after she left it. She expected to give up the campaign, but Millicent Garrett Fawcett, president of the NUWSS, wrote to her saying 'we regard you as a suffragist and we would like you to join us', and from then on she threw her lot in with the constitutionalists. In the short term this led to ructions with the Glasgow and West of Scotland Association, who had lost members to the militants and were now having Helen thrust down their throats as NUWSS organiser for Scotland, but all this settled down quickly.

Helen was able to utilise her talents to the full for the NUWSS. Unlike the WSPU, active mainly in the cities, the NUWSS formed branches all over the country. In summer 1908, using Louisa Lumsden's horse-drawn caravan, Helen toured the Borders, and in 1909 she borrowed it again to travel down the east coast from Aberdeen through Montrose, Brechin, Arbroath, Carnoustie, and Fife, then north again through Perth, Blairgowrie, Forfar, Edzell and Laurencekirk – a trek of some 300 miles. Apart from speaking all over the country, and helping to form new branches (in 1910 she was instrumental in setting up the North of Scotland Federation of Women's Suffrage Societies), she was also active in all the election and by-election campaigns. Later she worked as an organiser in London and other parts of England and also helped to build up branches in south Wales. In England she became known as 'the chieftainess because of her fine presence and air of command'.

When war broke out in 1914 Helen was recruited by the government and worked for the National War Savings Committee. She insisted on being paid the same rate as a man. During that period she was also seconded to the Board of Agriculture to make speeches urging women to go and work on the land, and to the Ministry of Food to urge voluntary rationing before it was imposed. In 1917, when the United States entered the war, the Women's Committee of the Council of National Defence in the USA asked the Foreign Office to send a woman speaker to spread the word about Britain's war efforts, and Helen crossed the Atlantic to do so. When she arrived she was interviewed by many journalists as the first woman to come to the United States on a war mission, and she was received by President Wilson at the White House. She travelled enormous distances, visiting over 40 states, and speaking '232 times in 228 days'. She was clearly a great success for, after a brief visit to France for first-hand observation, she was back in the USA for a second tour.

After the war Helen was employed in the civil service as Commissioner to the National War Savings Committee. In 1922 she was asked to stand as a Liberal candidate for Parliament, the first woman to be adopted as an official candidate in Scotland. She was offered a choice of two Glasgow seats, Shettleston and Govan, both firm Labour seats (it was a long time before any woman was offered a safe seat), and chose Govan as the more challenging because there was heavy unemployment in the shipyards. She knew 'there was a certain amount of amusement at the idea of a woman candidate', but after she had spoken to a number of meetings she 'was told they said, "She has a 'heid' on her".' She polled 9663 votes ('practically the combined total of the Conservative and Liberal candidates' votes at the 1918 election, and under much more difficult circumstances'), and enjoyed the experience enough to try a second time. This was in 1923, after another lecture tour of the USA, for Hamilton Division in Lanarkshire, another firm Labour seat, but that was a dirty fight which left a bitter taste. Her last political invitation was to fight Kelvingrove in Glasgow, but the Conservative candidate was a friend, and she knew that she would poll enough votes to cause him to lose his seat, so she declined and gave up party politics.

Helen then moved to London, earning money from freelance articles on women's issues, and sat on Kensington Council for seven years. She was a member of the International Women's Suffrage Alliance and was a delegate to all the major international conferences; for while in Britain women now had the vote, in most countries they did not. The 1926 conference, for example, was held in Paris, but French women did not get the vote until 1946. She enjoyed her freedom to travel and had not been tempted by marriage. However, she kept in touch with an old friend who had married and gone to Australia, where one of Helen's brothers was also living. His wife died, and he proposed to her on numerous occasions before she finally agreed and emigrated to Australia in 1938. She continued to speak on women's issues for the remainder of her life, and her book, *A Woman in a Man's World* (as Helen Moyes), was published in Australia in 1971. In 1975, aged 94, she was interviewed about her life and views.

*   *   *

Annot Wilkie or Robinson was another who started out in the WSPU and later switched to the NUWSS, though as a Labour activist her trajectory was different. Annot, born in 1874, and her sister Helen, were the daughters of John Wilkie, a Scottish laird's son who lost his money through unwise investment and set up in business as a draper in Montrose. This business was equally unsuccessful, and their mother, Catherine Jane Erskine, who had been a schoolmistress before her marriage, went back to teaching. This early life Annot later described as a 'starved poverty-stricken girlhood'.

With her mother as role model, Annot trained as a teacher in

Edinburgh; and in 1901 she was awarded the external degree of LLA (Lady Literate in Arts) by St Andrews University. She worked as a teacher in Fife and Dundee, where she came under the influence of the socialist and suffragist Agnes Husband (see Chapter 5). When a WSPU branch was set up in Dundee, Annot became its first secretary. During this period she met Sam Robinson, a working-class Labour activist from Manchester, and in January 1908 she married him. In February of that year she was one of a number of WSPU members hidden in a furniture van in yet another attempt to force their way into the House of Commons, and she was sentenced to six months imprisonment in Holloway. She then went to live in Manchester and bore two daughters, Cathie in 1909 and Helen in 1911, whose godfather was Keir Hardie.

The birth of her two children may have briefly curtailed her activities, but more important perhaps was a disillusionment with the Pankhurst leadership and tactics, and particularly with the move away from the WSPU's Labour roots. Her sister, Helen, joined the Women's Freedom League and became the Dundee branch secretary. Annot instead became active in the Women's Labour League. From 1912 onwards the new NUWSS policy of actively supporting Labour candidates in all by-elections brought Annot back into the suffrage movement. She was employed as an organiser for the election fighting fund, and apart from being involved in all the election campaigns in the Manchester area she was also active in Scotland during the by-elections in Midlothian and South Lanark.

Annot's allegiance to the NUWSS did not survive the outbreak of war, for as a pacifist she was one of those who resigned and helped to found the Women's International League for Peace and Freedom (WIL). During the war years she initiated the Women's War Interests Committee which helped to secure better conditions for young women munitions workers. In 1918 she became a full-time organiser for the Manchester branch of the WIL. In 1920 she went to Ireland as part of the WIL commission of enquiry into atrocities by the British Army, subsequently giving evidence before the American Commission for Ireland. She became vice-chairman of the Labour Party in Manchester and twice unsuccessfully contested difficult seats for Manchester City Council.

Annot's marriage was a disaster. In 1916, when she was in a state of physical collapse, she blamed this largely on 'the effect of a great emotional disappointment and disillusionment'. In 1919 she wrote to her sister that her husband was out working most of the time; when at home 'he smokes, spits and drinks'. It was she who supported the children, constantly fearing that they would suffer the poverty of her own childhood. Her fears became closer to reality in 1922 when, as a result of the economic slump, the WIL could no longer afford to employ her full time. She embarked on a two-month lecture tour of the United States, and helped to organise a WIL conference in Amsterdam, but in the end she was forced back into teaching. She died in 1925 of heart failure during an operation, and her friends in the WIL opened a memorial fund for the education of her daughters, which gave offence to her husband.

Ellen Wilkinson, Annot Robinson's obituarist, wrote that she 'had an exquisite sense of the ridiculous and a sharp tongue that was not infrequently used at the expense of powerful people whom she might perhaps have been wiser to conciliate'. She was 'a big woman and a powerful personality'.

* * *

After such apparently temperamental and quarrelsome women, it is a relief to describe someone of formidable intellect and firm principles, who achieved an immense amount professionally and as a feminist campaigner, without incurring enmity. (Jessie) Chrystal Macmillan was born in Edinburgh in 1872, the second child and only girl in a family of nine. Her father, John Macmillan, Master of the Edinburgh Merchant Company, a wealthy and successful businessman, was supportive, and Chrystal held her own amongst her brothers. Her mother, Jessie Chrystal Finlayson, died when she was young. John married again – the children's German governess.

St Leonard's School in St Andrews, founded to provide girls with an equivalent academic education to boys, has been mentioned earlier in connection with Louisa Lumsden. Chrystal went to board there in 1888 and was remembered as 'a tall, shy girl with a long brown pigtail and a strong bent for mathematics'. She became head of her house, and in her third year head of the school, so her shyness must have been quickly overcome.

When she left St Leonard's in 1891 Chrystal was awarded an open scholarship to Girton, Cambridge, but she refused it. According to one version she did so because she was needed at home; according to another she was determined to be one of the first women to enter Edinburgh University. In October 1892 she was indeed one of that pioneer band. She took a first class degree in mathematics and natural philosophy in 1896 and a second class MA in mental and moral philosophy in 1900, and followed this up with a period of study at Berlin University.

Back in Edinburgh, Chrystal became involved in the suffrage movement, as an executive committee member of the NUWSS and a vice-president of the Edinburgh National Society (later she was chairman of the Scottish Federation as well). In 1906 she became honorary secretary and treasurer of the newly-formed Committee of Women Graduates of the Scottish Universities (Parliamentary Franchise), along with Elsie Inglis and three other women, all graduates and thereby full members of the General Council of Edinburgh University. From 1868 the four universities of Scotland elected two members to parliament; the term 'person' rather than 'man' was used in the relevant statute, and when the women graduates were refused voting papers in the contested election of 1906 they formed a committee – and raised the money – to fight the universities' refusal before the Court of Session. They lost, and also lost an appeal the following year, but they took the case on to the House of Lords where it was heard in November 1908. The women garnered great publicity because Chrystal pleaded the case herself, presenting for several hours without interruption the legal arguments about why the term 'person' in the statute should be interpreted as including women. The final verdict was inevitably a defeat, but the favourable press coverage of her speech must have caused many to question why such a woman was considered incapable of voting.

Chrystal became a heroine to all three suffrage organisations in Scotland and was a guest of honour at several meetings. In 1909, under the auspices of the Scottish University Women's Suffrage Union (whose honorary secretary she became), she spoke all over the north of Scotland, in Caithness and Sutherland, as well as in Orkney and Shetland – no easy trip, for apart from the distances involved, steamers were irregular, making it difficult to arrange meetings. The nucleus of a society already existed in Shetland, but it was Chrystal's visit to Orkney that triggered the formation of the Orcadian Women's Suffrage Association.

As a staunch Liberal, the NUWSS election fighting fund to support the Labour Party may not have been easy for her to stomach, but she accepted the need for its existence and subscribed to it. In 1913 she was chairman of the NUWSS suffrage 'pilgrimage', and was a speaker (along with Louisa Lumsden) in London at the end of it. She wrote two pamphlets, *The Struggle for Political Liberty*, published by the Women's Press in 1909, and *Facts versus Fancies on Woman Suffrage* published by the NUWSS in 1914. By this time she was also active in the wider suffrage scene, becoming honorary secretary and vice-president of the International Women's Suffrage Alliance in 1913.

Chrystal's international outlook made her a committed pacifist, and she was one of the initiators of the International Peace Conference that met at The Hague in 1915. North Sea ferries had closed, so most of the British delegates (like Annot Robinson) were unable to attend, but Chrystal was one of three British women already in Holland. There were about 1500 women present, and on the last day Chrystal was one of four envoys appointed to carry the message of peace to neutral governments. They were received by the King of Norway and the President of the United States, and Chrystal went on to Canada to found a peace group there. In 1919 she was secretary of the Zürich

Women's International Congress and remained an active member of the Women's International League for Peace and Freedom throughout her life.

After the war Chrystal lived in London, and in 1923 was one of the first women to be called to the Bar. In that same year she was a founder of the Open Door Council which sought equal employment opportunities for women, and in 1929 she was a founder member and president of Open Door International. Later she was a committee member of the National Union of Societies for Equal Citizenship and an honorary vice-president of the Edinburgh Equal Citizenship Society. Her one attempt – in 1935 – to enter parliament as a Liberal candidate (in Edinburgh in 1935) was unsuccessful, but her legal knowledge enabled her to give expert advice on statutes relating to feminist issues. Her most active campaign was to secure the retention of British nationality for women married to foreign nationals (an issue not resolved until long after her death).

Chrystal Macmillan died in 1937. One obituary summed up her character thus: 'Her colleagues held her in high esteem, respecting her integrity, her fairness in argument, her ability, passion for justice, and utter lack of self-seeking.' In contrast to some of the suffragettes for whom the few years of struggling for the vote represented the high point of their lives, Chrystal Macmillan continued to campaign for total equality for women, while practising full-time as a barrister. She was, in effect, an archetypal 'constitutionalist', for whom the vote represented only one strand in the campaign for justice for women.

Chapter 4
The Women's
Social and Political Union

MARY Phillips, born in 1880, the daughter of a doctor working in Glasgow, went to work as an organiser for the Glasgow and West of Scotland Association for Women's Suffrage in 1904. She was therefore already part of the movement before the Pankhursts came on the scene, but the new-style militant campaigning made an immediate appeal to her, and indeed she later said that her period of work for a constitutionalist society made her aware of the futility of the older methods. Initially she must also have felt more at home with the Labour associations of the Women's Social and Political Union (WSPU) – before Christabel Pankhurst abandoned them – than with the Liberal ideology of the Glasgow Association, for Mary was a keen socialist and wrote a column in the Glasgow Labour journal, *Forward*. But her main loyalty from then on was to the Pankhursts. When the breakaway group that became the Women's Freedom League protested against the dictatorial style of leadership, Mary wrote: 'We owe the very existence of our Union, to the originality and courage of its founder, Mrs Pankhurst, whose untiring zeal in the cause of womanhood has led her to give herself wholly to it.'

Mary was one of the first Scottish WSPU members to be arrested and imprisoned (for six weeks) in Holloway; along with Annot Robinson she hid in a furniture van as part of a WSPU attempt to enter the House of Commons in February 1908. After her release she wrote to Annot that she had found imprisonment a 'peaceful time, with no worry .... One had nothing but affectionate farewells to remember of the friends outside, & nothing but love to cheer one from one's fellow-prisoners'. She found by-election campaigning in Scotland far more traumatic. The WSPU policy of opposing all Liberal candidates, even those in favour of women's suffrage, made no sense to the public at large, so the suffragettes were 'made a target for jeers and insults such as I never expected to hear from the lips of Scottish men and women, and such as, I fear, have permanently lowered my opinion of my compatriots'. Of the three forms of 'baptism' which every suffragette had to go through – to be thrown out of a cabinet minister's meeting, to go to prison, and to fight in a by-election – she reckoned that 'the last is by far the hardest of all'.

Mary was even more disillusioned after the Dundee by-election. Having lost his seat in Manchester, Winston Churchill was selected for the safe seat of Dundee, where the Liberal majority at the General Election had been 5000. His victory could never have been in doubt, but Mary, along with some other suffragettes, were convinced that he could be defeated and were encouraged by the enthusiastic, supportive crowds who listened to the suffrage speakers. So when Churchill won by 2700 votes Mary's opinion of her countrymen was again 'permanently lowered'. The suffragettes had reminded their audiences

> ... of the traditions of Scotland, of the fights for freedom in which our forefathers led, and in which our foremothers were never found behind the men of England in striking a blow for justice for women! How we have sought to stir their pride and their patriotism in these matters, and by asking them never to allow it to be said that Scotland was a dumping ground for England's second hand Goods!

(Helen Fraser was more perceptive in realising that Scots' 'Liberalism is a religion to them, and to vote against their party for us they consider too much to ask'.)

On 30 June 1908 Mary took part in another WSPU demonstration in London and was sentenced to three months' imprisonment in Holloway, making her the longest-serving suffragette prisoner. When she was released in September the WSPU organised a 'fine Scottish welcome' for her, with tartan and bagpipes, the kind of publicity stunt they did so well, and which the press lapped up. By this time Mary had become a paid organiser for the WSPU and as ardent a devotee as Christabel and Emmeline Pankhurst could have hoped for. At the beginning of 1909, after the latter were released from prison, Mary wrote in *Forward*, 'Dear, brave, noble women! As long as we live, we shall try to show, by every means in our power, the affection and gratitude we bear you'. Such cloying sentiments were not expressed by other Scottish WSPU members.

Once she became a paid organiser Mary spent nearly all of the following years in England, travelling from town to town wherever she was sent. She was imprisoned in Exeter in 1909 and went on hunger strike, but when she wrote to Christabel Pankhurst that she would like to take part in further militant activity and court prison for the cause, the latter replied that she must do no such thing: it was the 'voluntary workers' who were to make the protests, 'which of course you will organise'. Mary did, however, undergo at least one further period of imprisonment, in 1912, for an attempted assault on the Prime Minister, Asquith, though she was released after her fine was paid.

Mary received many appreciative and supportive letters from Christabel and Emmeline Pankhurst over the years, but in July 1913, far from being rewarded for her loyal service, she was dismissed from her position as organiser in Plymouth, with four weeks' salary in lieu of notice, followed by a derogatory letter from Christabel about her abilities as an organiser. This was a period of schism in the WSPU, and Mary immediately joined Sylvia Pankhurst, who had also been ejected from the WSPU, as an organiser for her East London Federation of Suffragettes. Having remained all her life what she described as 'extreme Left', she would have felt at home in that organisation. When the Pankhursts abandoned the suffrage cause after the outbreak of war, Mary joined the breakaway United Suffragists. In later years she was involved with the Suffragette Fellowship, which in about 1960 published her pamphlet, *The Militant Suffrage Campaign in Perspective*. Mary Phillips died in 1969. Her parents had moved to Cornwall soon after she herself left Scotland, and she does not appear to have kept up any Scottish connections.

* * *

Another Scotswoman whose activities were centred in England was Marion Wallace-Dunlop. Born in 1865 Marion was an artist who exhibited at the Royal Academy and also an illustrator of two books (*Fairies, Elves, and Bower Babies* and *The Magic Fruit Garden,* both published in 1899). She did not forget her Scottish origins, describing herself in 1909 as 'a direct descendant of the mother of William Wallace', but her most memorable action was as the first suffragette hunger striker in Holloway Prison. In June 1909 she stencilled an extract from the Bill of Rights on the wall of St Stephen's Hall in the House of Commons: 'It is the right of the subject to petition the King, and all commitments and prosecution for such petitions are illegal.' Denied the status of a political prisoner in Holloway she went on hunger strike and was released after 91 hours of fasting. This initiative earned her the approbation of the Pankhursts and was adopted as WSPU policy. Marion remained active in the movement (in England) throughout the pre-war years, and in 1928 she was a pallbearer at Emmeline Pankhurst's funeral.

* * *

As another WSPU paid organiser, Lillias Mitchell also spent some of the pre-war years in England, but her home was always in Edinburgh. Lillias, born in 1884, went to a suffrage meeting with her mother to hear Emmeline Pankhurst speak. 'Never shall I forget the blazing warmth of that meeting,' she wrote, 'we felt completely lifted out of ourselves, joined the society there and then and went home walking it seemed on air.' After that the things that had hitherto comprised her life, 'the hockey, reading, music clubs, violin lessons, even dances, seemed sheer nonsense when the Vote had yet to be won'. In the years that followed 'everything else was gradually swamped and I lived and moved and seemed to have my being in working for votes for women'. Although her mother was fully supportive, her father and brothers were not, and arguments raged. It must have been a relief to leave home and become involved in the movement full time.

Lillias' 'first real and horrid plunge into militancy' was as part of a march to the House of Commons in London, involving a 'terrible *mêleé* with the police', and concluding with a period of imprisonment in Holloway Prison.

In 1911 and 1912 she was the WSPU organiser in Aberdeen. In March 1912 the WSPU organised their most dramatic protest to date, a three-day window-smashing raid in London, causing hundreds of pounds of damage, and resulting in over 200 arrests. Lillias was one of the Scots contingent and remembered that the very thought of it 'made me shake from head to foot'.

But she knew what she had to do, and she was sentenced to four months' imprisonment in Holloway as a result. The suffragette prisoners were instructed to go on hunger strike in protest against the jailing of Mrs Pankhurst. Lillias was terrified of being forcibly fed, knowing that her heart had been weakened by a childhood bout of scarlet fever, 'and I felt sure that I would die – which at that time was unthinkable and awful'. When the time came she was so paralysed with fear that she put up a poor fight and so some of the liquid food got into her throat, which she felt as a defeat and cowardice. Mrs Pankhurst was released the next day, but Lillias felt a failure. She had hoped for an early release, but three months later she was still there and the prisoners learned that Mrs Pankhurst was returning to prison and they were all again to go on hunger strike. This time she was determined to fight until the end, and after winning her first battle she was released the following day.

After a short holiday with her mother, whose support buoyed her up enormously, Lillias returned to her post in Aberdeen. On one occasion she and a companion replaced all the marker flags at Balmoral Golf Course with flags painted with the WSPU colours and attached messages about the forcible feeding of suffragettes and votes for women. Later she pounced on Asquith, the Prime Minister, when he was playing golf at Dornoch, though charges were not pressed.

Lillias was then sent to be organiser at Newcastle and subsequently Birmingham. Early in 1914 she and another suffragette placed a home-made bomb in a railway station. In May of that year she was arrested for causing a breach of the peace, went on hunger strike at Winson Green Prison, was released on licence and then re-arrested under the Cat and Mouse Act.

Lillias was a member of the Edinburgh Women's Citizens Association after the war, so her commitment to feminism obviously remained firm. She worked as secretary to the Edinburgh and South Area of the Young Women's Christian Association before dying of a heart condition in 1940.

*　*　*

Two sisters who were also detained in Holloway Prison after the 1912 window-smashing raid were Frances and Margaret McPhun. Their father, John, was a timber merchant, the police magistrate of the city of Glasgow, and one of the founders of the People's Palace. Margaret, born in 1876, graduated with an MA degree in Psychology from Glasgow University; while Frances, born in 1880, was also a Glasgow University graduate, with an MA in Political Economy. The sisters both had a social conscience, working at the Queen Margaret College Settlement. From 1906 to 1908 Margaret was honorary treasurer of the North Kelvinside and Maryhill Liberal Association, but her politics then moved to the left, for between 1911 and 1913 she was a regular contributor to the Glasgow socialist journal, *Forward*. Both sisters joined the WSPU in 1909 (prior to that Margaret had been Glasgow convenor for the Scottish University Women's Suffrage Union). Frances was involved in organising the 'Pageant of Famous Scottish Women' for a procession held in Edinburgh in 1909, was joint organiser of the WSPU exhibition held in Glasgow in 1910, and was honorary secretary of the Glasgow WSPU between 1911 and 1912. Margaret was press secretary for the WSPU in Scotland from 1912 to 1914.

During their spell in Holloway in 1912 they went on hunger strike and were forcibly fed. In personal letters Margaret wrote of the horrors of the experience, though nothing of those horrors was allowed into the poem she wrote that was included in *Holloway Jingles,* published by the Glasgow branch of the WSPU in 1913. She also contributed to *Votes for Women* and *The Suffragette.* The sisters were amongst the most active WSPU members in Scotland (and went to London for all the major processions there), but it does not appear that either of them took part in the arson or bombing attacks that characterised the last period of WSPU activity in Britain.

Little is known of Frances' activities after the war (she lived until 1940), but Margaret continued her involvement in feminist campaigning. She was a member of the Glasgow Women's Citizens' Association and secretary of the Scottish Council of Women's Citizens' Associations. She also belonged to other feminist organisations, like the Open Door Council and the Scottish Council for Women's Trades and Careers. In the 1930s she and her sister gave a large house in Callender to the Glasgow Guild of Aid, to be used as a holiday home for the disadvantaged. Margaret McPhun lived until 1960.

* * *

So far, the WSPU members in this chapter all underwent periods of imprisonment in England – but not in Scotland. Of course, in the early years most of the demonstrations resulting in arrests took place in London. But when, in October 1909, an attempt was made to storm the doors of the Kinnaird Hall in Dundee where Winston Churchill was to speak, all but one of the women involved were English. Courting arrest in a place where one was 'kent' was much harder than doing so in the anonymity of London. The Scottish woman in question was not a young firebrand, but a married woman with three children – Mrs Helen Archdale.

Helen, born at Nenthorn, Roxburghshire in 1876, was the daughter of Alexander Russel, editor of *The Scotsman,* who had been an active supporter of Sophia Jex-Blake in her fight for women's medical education, and Helen De Lacy Evans, one of the students involved in that campaign. Not surprisingly, with such a background, Helen was educated at St Leonard's School in St Andrews. Subsequently she also attended sessions at St Andrews University. In 1901 she married Captain, later Lieutenant Colonel, Theodore Montgomery Archdale, who was stationed in India.

Helen returned from India in September 1908 and immediately joined the Women's Social and Political Union. As a result of her actions in Dundee in October 1909 she, along with four English women, was arrested for breach of the peace. They immediately went on hunger strike. At that time women were being forcibly fed in Newcastle, so Helen and her companions knew what was likely to be in store for them, but the Scottish authorities proved far more reluctant to resort to forcible feeding (that would come later), and all of the women were released after four days. Helen was said to have lost one and a half stone during that time.

In 1911 Helen moved to London and became the WSPU's prisoners' secretary, organising information and comforts. In December 1911 she herself received a sentence of two months' imprisonment in Holloway for window-breaking. Afterwards she continued to work for the WSPU, helping out in particular with *The Suffragette*. During the war she started a training farm for women agricultural workers, was a clerical worker with Queen Mary's Auxiliary Corps from 1917, and in 1918 worked in the Women's Department of the Ministry of National Service.

After the war Helen continued her feminist campaigning. In 1920 she was the first editor of a new journal, *Time and Tide* (with its unspoken sub-text 'wait for no man'). She was a founder member of the Open Door Council and Open Door International and was prominent in several other feminist organisations in the inter-war period. She contributed articles on feminist issues to *The Times*, *The Daily News*, *The Scotsman*, and other journals. The stereotype for WSPU members (unlike those of the NUWSS and WFL), of campaigning for the vote as a single-issue, is certainly inapplicable to Helen Archdale. Her daughter, Betty Archdale, who shared her outlook, became principal of the Women's College in the University of Sydney. Helen died in North London in December 1949.

*   *   *

From 1912 more Scottish suffragettes were willing to court arrest and imprisonment within Scotland. In November of that year, three women concealed themselves in the Music Hall in Aberdeen, where Lloyd George, Chancellor of the Exchequer at the time, was scheduled to speak. Explosive caps of the kind used for toy pistols were found in their possession, and it was alleged that they intended to cause mayhem and panic at the meeting. When the case came to court, the charge against them was breach of the peace, though all they had done was struggle against their captors. They were found guilty and sentenced to five days' imprisonment. On their release the *Dundee Advertiser* discovered that one of them, who called herself Marion Pollock, had taken a train to Dundee and belonged to that city. After tantalising readers with hints of who she might be, the paper then covered her public appearance at the Forresters' Hall. She was 36 year-old May Pollock Grant, the daughter of the minister of St Mark's parish church in Dundee.

May had gone to India in 1905, where she was a Church of Scotland missionary, having already spent the ten previous years doing missionary work at home. She was, she told her audience at Forresters' Hall, 'deeply, passionately, attached to the Auld Reformed Kirk o' the Realm'. She was aware that some of her audience 'had known her since she was a little girl .... Now she appeared on the platform as a gaol-bird!' To May the suffrage campaign was, in effect, an extension of missionary work, for she had 'heard the call of the oppressed, sweated betrayed women'. To have been jailed for involvement in such a movement was a matter of pride, not shame.

There is no suggestion that May Grant took part in any of the secret arson or bombing attacks in Scotland, but the form her militancy took arguably required a greater degree of courage because the fire-raisers did their best not to be caught, whereas to interrupt and heckle at public meetings invariably provoked a violent reaction. Again and again she underwent this treatment. After a meeting in Aberdeen in 1913, when she had clung to the railings, causing the stewards great difficulty in extricating her, she said that she did not think much of the argument that men should have the vote on the basis of their physical superiority, as it had taken six to eight of them to remove her the previous evening. Three nights later, at a meeting in Perth City Hall, she and another woman 'were bundled out screaming and struggling, the audience standing in a state of much excitement'. The mere fact of a woman shouting out in a public meeting brought out something atavistic in crowds, and whatever she might have said about it, to subject herself to such violent hostility time and time again cannot have been lightly undertaken. She also spoke in public, in spite of the fact that suffragettes by this time invariably attracted hostile crowds. And she flooded the *Dundee Advertiser* with letters about why women should be granted the vote. She was a formidable adherent to the cause.

When war broke out in 1914, May worked with a Voluntary Aid Detachment Driver in Dundee until her father's death in 1916. According to her obituary she then did 'war work' in Gretna, Waltham Abbey and Greetland near Halifax, before joining the women's police service, rising from constable to sub-inspector in the munitions factories. Later she took up police duties in London.

May Grant continued to be interested in politics and twice stood as a Liberal candidate in English constituencies. In the 1930s she became interested in Christian Science and spent the rest of her life as a practitioner and healer. During World War II she did civil defence work during the London Blitz. She moved to Seaford, Sussex in 1943, and later went to Tunbridge Wells, where she died in 1957.

*   *   *

Of course, not all WSPU members were at liberty to spend time in prison, or even to make public spectacles of themselves, especially if they were working-class women and had to earn a living. According to Jessie Stephen, the WSPU had many working-class members, but because they had to protect their anonymity we know nothing about most of them. The facts about Jessie are known because she remained active in the trades union movement throughout her long life and was interviewed in the 1970s.

Jessie Stephen was the eldest of eleven children in a closely-knit Glasgow family. Her father, a tailor, joined the Independent Labour Party (ILP) at its formation, so she grew up in a committed socialist household. She hoped to become a teacher, but the family could not support her training, so she went into domestic service instead. At the age of 16 (in about 1909) she joined both the ILP and the WSPU, and in her spare time was highly active in both. In January 1912 she was the youngest member of the Glasgow delegation that formed part of the WSPU Deputation of Working Women to Lloyd George.

At the beginning of 1913 the favoured form of 'secret' militancy in Scotland was attacks on pillar boxes. Acid was dropped into the boxes, destroying most of the letters within them, as part of the 'guerrilla' warfare being waged by the WSPU. It may have alienated public sympathy, but it was virtually risk-free, particularly if, like Jessie, one was dressed in the muslin apron, black dress and cap and cuffs of a domestic servant while doing this. Jessie never encountered suspicion and had no compunction about carrying out these attacks which, she said, were organised 'with a military precision'.

When war broke out Jessie could not follow the jingoistic line of Emmeline and Christabel Pankhurst, and in fact she spent the war years working for Sylvia Pankhurst's East London Federation of Suffragettes. She also worked as an ILP organiser in East London. After the war, having failed to be selected as an ILP parliamentary candidate, she was elected as a Labour borough councillor for Bermondsey in November 1922. She remained in England, a committed socialist, pacifist and Trade Unionist.

* * *

Catherine Blair had four children to bring up, so she did not risk prison, but she was one of Scotland's strongest advocates of militancy, both as a speaker and as a writer of numerous letters to newspapers. Born Catherine Shields in 1872, the daughter of an East Lothian farmer, she married Thomas Blair in 1894, setting up home at Hoprig Mains Farm, Gladsmuir. Apart from defending militancy, she also provided a refuge for suffragette prisoners released under the Cat and Mouse Act. Her husband fully supported her, resigning his vice-presidency of the local Liberal party because of the government's treatment of the suffrage question.

In 1917 Catherine Blair founded the first Scottish Women's Rural Institute. In spite of its later image, to set up rural networks of women was at the time something new and bold. In 1919 Catherine Blair created the Mak'Merry Pottery. She died in 1946 and was still remembered in Edinburgh in the 1990s.

* * *

Elizabeth Finlayson Gauld, who had been active as a speaker (mostly for the Women's Freedom League) from 1910, took part in the WSPU's window-smashing raid in March 1912, when she was 59. But she was not imprisoned, for when she came before the court she stated that she was the matron of an orphanage in Edinburgh and therefore would give an undertaking that she would not break the law again. This did not curtail her involvement in the movement. She spoke at every major Scottish event, and when forcible feeding was carried out in Scotland she was one of those who agitated most strongly against the practice. During and after the war, she too was involved in the Scottish Women's Rural Institute.

In later years she was an invalid. As far as the Suffragette Fellowship was concerned, a period of imprisonment marked the true suffragette, and Elizabeth Finlayson Gauld was hurt not to be invited to the unveiling of Emmeline Pankhurst's statue in 1930.

*   *   *

Amongst those who did take risks and undergo imprisonment were some professional women, particularly doctors. One of the first women graduates in medicine from Glasgow University, in 1894 (at the age of 22), was (Elizabeth) Dorothea Lynas, who then joined the staff of Glasgow's Royal Samaritan Hospital for Women. Several years later she married Rev. William Chalmers Smith, minister of Glasgow's Calton Church, and bore him six children, which would have left her little time for suffrage activity. (Her sister Jane was a member of the WSPU in Glasgow.) But in July 1913 Dorothea took part in the arson campaign and was found, along with Ethel Moorhead (see Chapter 6), inside a Glasgow house with fire-lighting equipment.

While on remand in Duke Street Prison, Dorothea Chalmers Smith went on hunger strike; she was released under the Cat and Mouse Act after five days. She did not return to prison when her licence expired, but she was located and tried, and in October she was sentenced to eight months' imprisonment. This sentence caused uproar in court when many of the women present started throwing missiles at the Bench. (Dorothea's sister, Jane, was arrested after this affray.) Dorothea again went on hunger strike and was released under licence on 20 October, but did not return when due back on the 27th. She remained in her home in Glasgow, and the police kept a 24 hour watch on the house, much to the dismay of Rev. William Chalmers Smith. On 19 November Dorothea escaped by changing clothes with a friend visiting her for tea; the suspicions of one of the detectives had been aroused, but too late to stop the escape. She was not recaptured.

The Smith marriage did not survive. Dorothea eventually left her husband, taking her four daughters with her; the two sons remained with their father who forbade them to see their mother. Dorothea's spell of imprisonment did not do any harm to her career in the long term; she resumed practising as a doctor, and though she died in 1944, as late as 1990 she was still remembered in Glasgow as a wonderful doctor and a remarkable woman.

* * *

Alice Ker was another Scottish doctor (and mother) who belonged to the WSPU and was imprisoned, though in England rather than Scotland. Alice was the niece of Flora and Louisa Stevenson (see Chapter 2). Of the six Stevenson sisters, two of them married, and Alice's mother, the eldest, was one of them. Alice's father was Edward Stewart Ker, Free Church minister in Deskford, Banffshire, and Alice, born in 1853, was the eldest of eleven children. Apart from visits to her aunts in Edinburgh, Alice later wrote that her own mother 'must have been a born feminist' for 'she always said that her boys should not have more chances than her girls, who should be brought up to earn their living like the boys'.

In 1872 Alice started to attend the university-standard classes for women in Edinburgh where she met the women students led by Sophia Jex-Blake who were fighting for medical training for women, and she decided that she too wanted to be a doctor. It was not yet possible to obtain a degree in England or Scotland, but when the Irish colleges opened their examinations to women in 1879 she was awarded the Licentiate of the King's and Queen's College of Physicians, Ireland. She then shared a practice in Edinburgh with Sophia Jex-Blake for a year, spent a year studying at Berne University (paid for by Aunt Louisa), worked as a house surgeon in the children's hospital in Birmingham, ran a practice in Leeds, and by 1887 was back in Edinburgh with plans to set up her own practice. Instead, the following year, she married her cousin, Edward Ker, a shipping merchant in Liverpool, and settled with him in Birkenhead.

Alice practised as a doctor in Birkenhead and in 1891 published a book entitled *Motherhood: A Book for Every Woman*. She had by this time two daughters of her own. During the 1890s she also became involved in the local branch of the NUWSS. In May 1907 her husband died unexpectedly. Her change of heart from 'suffragist' to 'suffragette' took place in the course of 1909. It was a gradual one, for she was part of a network of women who disapproved of the new militant methods, but ultimately she was so convinced by the WSPU's tactics that she took part in the March 1912 window-smashing raid in London and was imprisoned in Holloway as a result. She was asked to resign one of her medical positions, but refused to do so. She wrote to her daughters from prison about her strong belief in what she was doing and her elder daughter, Margaret, was caught setting fire to a pillar box in Liverpool in October 1912, sentenced to three months' imprisonment, and narrowly escaped expulsion from Liverpool University.

In November 1916 Dr Alice Ker moved to London and continued to practise as a GP in Golders Green. She died in 1943 at the age of 90.

*   *   *

The final woman in this chapter, Helen Crawfurd, who left an unpublished autobiography, followed different paths from any of the others. She was born Helen Jack in the Gorbals parish of Glasgow in 1877, the fourth child of a family of seven, her father a master baker. When Helen was a young child he bought a bakery in Ipswich, Suffolk, so Helen's early life and education were in the south of England. In 1894 the family returned to Glasgow, which Helen later wrote 'was a horror to a young person coming from a clean country town like Ipswich'. As a result of the shipbuilding industry the city was booming, but the 'skilled creators of the city's wealth were living in squalor, in hovels unfit for human beings. I began to think that there must be something wrong with a system that could allow this'. But as part of a very conservative family, if she ever heard a soap-box speaker mention the word 'socialism' she 'fled as from the devil!'

Evangelical religion was endemic in Glasgow at that time, and Helen's parents, already intensely religious, were swept up in this. Her father discovered Brownfield Church where the Rev. Alexander Montgomerie Crawfurd 'preached the real Gospel of Christ'. According to Helen, he 'had a fine voice, and a dramatic delivery' and 'would have made a wonderful actor'. But his church was sparsely attended – not, it would appear, because 'he truly believed in the literal interpretation of the Scriptures', but because he held strong views on temperance and on militarism, which alienated some of his members. But Helen's family admired his strong principles, and Helen was active in the church, going to prayer meetings and Sunday School, helping to start a choir, and also taking part in evangelical meetings.

Helen had no idea that she was arousing personal interest in the minister of Brownfield Church until he suddenly asked her to marry him. 'I thought he had suddenly gone mad for he was so much older than I was, that this idea had never entered my head.' (She does not specify his age in her autobiography, but she refers to a grown-up daughter from a first marriage with whom she later became good friends, and whose own daughters later came to suffrage meetings with her.) She naturally refused him, but he persisted in asking. What eventually persuaded her, apparently, was not a growing fondness for him but 'the suggestion that this might be God's plan for me, and that I would be trained as a missionary'. In 1898 they were married. It turned out not to be 'easy' for either of them, though Helen's 'sense of duty and reverence for the man of God, together with my own strong religious belief that this was on the path ordained by Him made life possible'. At the same time a growing respect for Keir Hardie made her less intolerant of socialists, and having 'always resented any suggestion of the inferiority of women', she found her feminism growing as well. Gradually 'it seemed all wrong that the religious people should be so much concerned about heaven and a future life, and so little concerned with the present, where God's creatures were living in slums, many of them owned by Churches, amidst poverty and disease'.

In 1910 she joined the WSPU at a meeting in Rutherglen. She became a speaker and felt that the main advantage she gained was that it compelled her 'to study economic conditions in order to speak effectively'. She also read socialist literature for the first time and found it very persuasive. Helen was part of the Glasgow contingent that took part in the window-breaking raid in London in March 1912.

On the Sunday before making up her mind to undertake this she went to church and prayed that she would get a message during the sermon. Little did her husband realise that his sermon on Christ making a whip of cords and chasing the money-changers out of the temple would confirm to Helen that her 'participation in the raid was right. If Christ could be Militant so could I'. She was fortunate in one respect: her part in the window-smashing was on the first day, when prison sentences were quite lenient.

Between 1912 and 1914 Helen's political education and role as a speaker for the WSPU continued. Her speeches 'always had socialist content, although I was far from being politically clear. Mine was at that time, a sort of Christian Socialism'. In March 1914 Mrs Pankhurst, out on licence under the Cat and Mouse Act, was smuggled into a hall in Glasgow for a public meeting. Helen was a member of her body-guard, and the police badly botched the arrest, causing mayhem and injuries to a number of women. As a protest the next day Helen broke two windows at an army recruiting office in Glasgow, was arrested and sentenced to a month's imprisonment. This seems small beer at a time when suffragettes were burning and bombing all over the country, but it appeared a reasonable protest to Helen (she thought that others would follow her lead, but none did), and a picket was organised out-side Duke Street Prison where Helen was hunger-striking. After eight days she was released under licence, which meant she was to return when recovered. She was re-arrested, went on another hunger strike and was again released under licence.

Helen's husband died at the end of May 1914. During that summer forcible feeding was being carried out in Perth Prison, and suffragettes were carrying out 24 hour vigils outside the walls. King George and Queen Mary were touring Scotland at this time, so inevitably there were fears of what the suffragettes might do and thus a strong police presence in Perth. Helen was so keen to see the King and Queen that she got another woman to substitute for her in the picket. The police had left her alone when she was making speeches, but presumably they thought she had designs on the Royal couple, for they re-arrested her under the Cat and Mouse Act and put her in Perth Prison. After five days of hunger-striking she was again released. There was no attempt to feed her forcibly, for, unlike the other suffragettes who by this time always went on hunger *and* thirst strike, Helen drank water, and because the women being forcibly fed were those who had committed acts of arson; breaking a couple of windows was hardly in that category.

The outbreak of war in August 1914 signalled the end of militancy, but as we have seen raised issues of conscience amongst the women who had been involved in the cause. Although Helen was one of the founders of the Women's Peace Crusade in 1916 and founded a branch of the Women's International League for Peace and Freedom, she later said that she was never a pacifist. She 'was an International socialist with a profound hatred of war with all its ghastly cruelty and waste', and as an Independent Labour Party speaker she 'travelled throughout the country, exposing the Armament Rings and the war makers and urging the women to revolt against the sacrifice of their sons'. By 1920 she considered the ILP not nearly radical enough and joined the Communist Party instead, travelling to Russia to meet Lenin and other leaders. She was elected to the Party executive and put in charge of their work among women. In the 1930s she was honorary secretary of an anti-fascist committee in Renfrew. Later she became Dunoon's first woman town councillor. She apparently remained a committed Marxist until her death in 1954.

* * *

This does not conclude the stories of the WSPU suffragettes about whom anything is known, for there was a 'hard core' of a few women who were responsible for most of the serious damage to property at the end, who were forcibly fed, and about whom there is much to write. Their inclusion here would unbalance the chapter. We will therefore return to them in Chapter 6.

Chapter 5
The Women's Freedom League

THE Women's Freedom League (WFL) did not have a large number of members as the NUWSS did, and those members did not, on the whole, seek publicity the way WSPU members did. Also, historians have paid less attention to the organisation, and therefore it has been harder to find out much about these women. For example, Alexia B Jack was the honorary secretary of the WFL's Edinburgh branch throughout the pre-war period, and was also honorary secretary and treasurer of the Scottish Council of the WFL, as well as being one of the Scottish representatives on the National Executive Council. She was born in 1863, died in 1949, and was a teacher, proud of the fact that by 1913 she held the position of 'second master' in an elementary school, one of only three women to have reached that level of seniority in Edinburgh. When war broke out she worked under the aegis of the WFL to look after the interests of women in agriculture, until her health broke down in 1915. After 1918 she became the first honorary secretary and a vice-president of the Edinburgh Women's Citizens Association. And that is all that is known of her. Fortunately there are more facts available on a few other key figures in the WFL.

* * *

Dundee's Agnes Husband was in her forties before she became politically active. She was born in Tayport in about 1853, the daughter of a master mariner. Whether out of necessity or simply a desire for independence, she set herself up in business as a dressmaker. The origins of her socialism are not known, but by the end of the nineteenth century she was standing for election to the parish council as a socialist candidate. Initially unsuccessful, in 1901 she was elected as one of the first two women members. She took her duties seriously, attending some 80 meetings a year. Subsequently she was elected onto the school board. She was also actively involved with the Distress Committee, the Departmental Committee on Industrial and Reformatory Schools, the National Health Insurance Committee, and the Juvenile Advisory Committee. In her obituary she was described as 'a pioneer in asserting the claims of women and their competence to participate in the administration of public affairs', and also 'a pioneer in more humane methods of treatment of the poor and in education and care of children'.

Her involvement in the suffrage movement pre-dated the creation of the Women's Social and Political Union, for she was present at the inaugural meeting of the Dundee and East Fife Women's Suffrage Committee (which came under the NUWSS umbrella) in December 1904. But militancy made an immediate appeal, and she joined the WSPU. This did not last long, for someone accustomed to working democratically through committee structures was hardly going to accept orders from the Pankhurst autocracy, so she joined the breakaway Women's Freedom League. In 1909 she became president of the Dundee branch of the WFL, and she was a Scottish representative on the League's National Executive Committee. When Winston Churchill agreed to accept a WFL deputation in October 1909 Agnes Husband was one of the two members to take part in this fruitless exercise.

After the war Agnes was a member of the executive committee of the Dundee Women's Citizens Association and continued her local government activities. In 1926, at the age of 74, she was awarded the Freedom of the City. Agnes Husband died three years later. As mentioned in Chapter 3, Annot Robinson was influenced by her both as a socialist and suffragist, and presumably she was a role model for others as well.

* * *

The other member of the WFL deputation to Churchill in 1909, and a very active participant in the suffrage struggle in Dundee, was Lila

Clunas. Born in Glasgow, she trained as a teacher at Moray House, Edinburgh, and then went to work in an elementary school in Dundee. When the militant suffrage movement came to Scotland in 1906 Lila immediately became involved, but when the WFL broke away she became one of the founders of its Dundee branch and was its secretary from 1908 to 1912. In August 1909 she became Dundee's first suffragette prisoner in Holloway Prison for trying to present a petition to the Prime Minister, Asquith. After her return home, a reporter from the *Advertiser* was fascinated to hear someone describe prison experiences as a matter of pride rather than shame.

While continuing to call itself a militant society, the WFL did not follow the WSPU's path into violence, confining itself to interrupting public meetings and to acts of civil disobedience. Lila addressed public meetings and frequently had letters published in the *Advertiser* defending even violent militancy (along with May Grant of the WSPU, her name would have been known to any reader of that paper in the years leading up to the war). And when forcible feeding was carried out in Perth Prison, Lila was in the town to speak at protest meetings.

In common with Agnes Husband, Lila was a member of the Labour Party, and she too became involved in local government. She was for many years (well into the 1940s) a member of the town council, with a particular interest in education, and a member of the school board. She never married but lived with a sister and younger brother. Three-quarters of a century later she was remembered as a 'quiet, small, kindly person'.

* * *

Two notable activists in Edinburgh were Agnes (Nannie) Henderson Brown and her sister Jessie. Nannie was the youngest of a family of two sons and two daughters. Their father was the proprietor of a number of fruiterer's shops in the city, and a man keenly interested in social and political reform. Nannie and Jessie were among the first women to be seen on bicycles in Scotland.

Flora Stevenson. With her sister Louisa (*see Notice of Annual Meeting, below*), she became involved in the suffrage struggle in 1867. The Stevenson sisters were amongst the most successful suffragists of the mid-nineteenth century.

Priscilla Bright McLaren. Born in 1815 into a family which was politically active in progressive causes, she was chosen as the first president of the Edinburgh National Society for Women's Suffrage in 1867.

Jane Taylour. Much admired by Priscilla Bright McLaren, Taylour was a confident public speaker who was praised for her 'tact, eloquence, and singularly lucid manner'. She had delivered 152 lectures in Scotland by 1873.

Notice of the Annual Meeting of the Edinburgh National Society for Women's Suffrage in 1901.

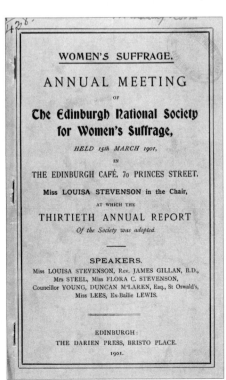

WOMEN'S SUFFRAGE.

ANNUAL MEETING

OF

The Edinburgh National Society
for Women's Suffrage,

HELD 15th MARCH 1901,

IN

THE EDINBURGH CAFÉ, 7o PRINCES STREET,

Miss LOUISA STEVENSON in the Chair,

AT WHICH THE

THIRTIETH ANNUAL REPORT

Of the Society was adopted.

SPEAKERS.

Miss LOUISA STEVENSON, Rev. JAMES GILLAN, B.D.,
Mrs STEEL, Miss FLORA C. STEVENSON,
Councillor YOUNG, DUNCAN M'LAREN, Esq., St Oswald's,
Miss LEES, Ex-Bailie LEWIS.

EDINBURGH:
THE DARIEN PRESS, BRISTO PLACE.
1901.

Above: A suffrage procession along Princes Street in Edinburgh, 1909.

Right: A 'fine Scottish welcome' to Mary Phillips in September 1908. After taking part in a WSPU (Women's Social and Political Union) demonstration in London on 30 June 1908, she was arrested and imprisoned in Holloway for three months – making her the longest-serving suffragette prisoner thus far. Upon her release, her friends laid on this impressive event – with tartan and bagpipes ensuring maximum publicity for the suffragette cause in the British press. (NMS)

Left: A demonstration held by Women's Freedom League members on Glasgow Green in 1909. The WFL suffragists lobbied political figures and public bodies to campaign for votes for women, restricting themselves to interrupting meetings and acts of civil disobedience, while the WSPU suffragettes (*group pictured below, with Mrs Pankhurst*) went on to use violent means to fight their cause.

Left: Anna Munro stands before a Women's Freedom League banner. She was the group's organiser between 1908 and 1912, and was instrumental in making the WFL successful in educating the public about women's rights.

Below: A celebratory home-coming after a spell in prison, the banner reads 'Released from Holloway To-day'.

Left: Anna Munro wearing prison dress in 1913, after holding an illegal suffrage meeting in Hyde Park.

Below: A female anti-slavery medal reads 'Am I Not a Woman and a Sister?' and Psalm II.3, 'Let us break their bands asunder and cast away their cords'.

Below left to right: Hunger strike medal given to one of the McPhun sisters (Frances and Margaret) after their spell in Holloway in 1912, during which they endured forcible feeding.

Suffragette banner

An original copy of 'Holloway Jingles', a songbook of verses published by the Glasgow branch of the WSPU in 1913.

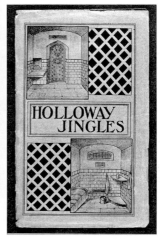

INSURANCE ACT PROTEST.

THE VOTE

THE ORGAN OF THE WOMEN'S FREEDOM LEAGUE

Vol. VIII. No. 196.   Registered at the General Post Office as a Newspaper.   FRIDAY, JULY 25, 1913.   ONE PENNY.

Edited by C. DESPARD.

OBJECTS: To secure for Women the Parliamentary vote as it is or may be granted to men; to use the power thus obtained to establish equality of rights and opportunities between the sexes, and to promote the social and industrial well-being of the community.

THE SCOTTISH SUFFRAGE DEPUTATION ARRIVING AT THE PRIME MINISTER'S HOUSE, 10, DOWNING STREET, LONDON, JULY 19, 1913.

NORTHERN MEN'S FEDERATION FOR WOMEN'S SUFFRAGE

GLASGOW

"NOW'S THE DAY AND NOW'S THE HOUR"

Above: The deputation to Prime Minister Asquith in June 1913 saw eminent male members of society from Scotland and the north of England travel to 10 Downing Street.

Far left: 'The Organ of the Women's Freedom League', *The Vote* records the deputation's arrival at 10 Downing Street. The headline is slightly misleading, however, as the group was turned away at the door.

Left: The group of men who made up the suffrage deputation was to be the forerunner of the Northern Men's Federation for Women's Suffrage.

One of the first women graduates in medicine from the University of Glasgow in 1894, Dorothea Chalmers Smith was caught with fire-lighting equipment inside a house with Ethel Moorhead (*below, right*), depicted in a cartoon from the *Wizard of the North* magazine, March 1912.

Above: One result of the arson campaign mounted by WSPU members in 1913 – Farington Hall in Dundee, burnt, featured in the *London Illustrated News* (May 24 1913).

Below, left: An artists portrayal of the infamous window-smashing raid held in London, from the *London Illustrated News* (9 March 1912). Organised by the WSPU, several Scottish women took part and were arrested for their actions, being detained in Holloway as a result.

Right: Eunice Murray, president of the Women's Freedom League, which continued to campaign for the vote during the war years. Author of a pamphlet called 'Woman – the New Discovery', her main concern was that new attitudes towards women who had previously been in subservient positions before the war should continue in the labour market when the fighting ended. In 1918 she became the first Scottish woman candidate to stand in a General Election.

Below: A street demonstration during World War I – women working from home while men were away at war.

GENERAL ELECTION, 1918.

Bridgeton Parliamentary Division.

Miss EUNICE G. MURRAY,
NON-PARTY CANDIDATE.

In 1910 and 1911 Nannie Brown's name featured in various reports about WFL activities in Edinburgh, ranging from heckling parliamentary candidates to arranging country dances for social events, and addressing open-air meetings.

In October 1912, in an attempt to capture the public's imagination with something new, a 400-mile suffrage march of was planned from Edinburgh to London, with signatures to be gathered on a petition to Asquith. It was not expected that most of the marchers would go the whole distance (only six did so), but they would join or leave at different points, with an open-air suffrage meeting to be held every evening (except Sunday), and talks given when requested at villages en route, culminating in a grand rally in London. After a rousing send-off from Charlotte Square – the *Daily Mail* estimated there were 10,000 spectators lining Princes Street – Nannie was one of those who set out with the intention of returning home after a few days, but she 'found the march was so intensely enjoyable' that she went all the way to London.

Nannie later described the five-week march. She felt proud that throughout the period 'we Marchers kept exactly to our Timetable':

After a walk of 14 to 18 miles, working all the time trying to get signatures to our Petition to Mr Asquith, from everyone we met on the road, it was no easy matter to turn out after the evening meal to conduct an open-air meeting, which usually lasted about two hours; yet each meeting was held at exactly the advertised hour, and we marched into London on the date, and at the exact hour, previously arranged.

The marchers were all dressed 'in russet brown tweed coats and skirts, with green ribbons on our hats, and green ties' and were known throughout the country as 'the Brown Women'. Of course, not everyone who was asked was willing to sign the petition. One Scotsman replied, 'Votes for women! I wid raither sign your death warrant'; and an Englishman responded, 'All that you say, be no doubt very true, but I has made it a rule in life never to sign nothin', and sign nothin' I never will'.

Two meetings (in Stamford and Peterborough) were broken up by rowdies, but otherwise all went peaceably, and the women met innumerable kindnesses along their route. In one village they were asked to take part in a debate on women's suffrage. The villagers were strongly anti-suffrage. One old man, rising to his feet with difficulty, and 'looking solemnly round the audience for a minute, said emphatically, "All I wants to hask is this, where is this to hend: it will hend with lydies gettin' into Parliament, and hall I says is Parliament aint no place for a lydy to be" and was then helped to his seat again, amid loud and prolonged applause'. The suffragettes were only allowed three minutes each to put their case, and they were utterly amazed to learn, when the votes were counted at the end, that 53 had voted against women's suffrage and 64 in favour, 'so that we had won our cause by 11 votes in this stronghold of the Antis!'

An unexpected consequence of Emily Wilding Davison's death after throwing herself in front of the King's horse at the Derby in June 1913 was a deputation to Prime Minister Asquith of a group of councillors, bailies, JPs, ministers, solicitors and barristers from Edinburgh, Glasgow and the north of England. Asquith would not listen to them, but a new organisation was born, the Northern Men's Federation for Women's Suffrage. Unlike the WSPU, which categorically refused to have any male members, there had always been a substantial minority of WFL members who welcomed male participation in the struggle, and such women, including Nannie and Jessie Brown, were crucial in forming the NMF. Nannie became honorary secretary of the Edinburgh branch, which continued campaigning even during the war years.

After the war Nannie was involved in setting up the Scottish Women's Rural Institutes. Her suffrage march certainly did not put her off walking, for she and Jessie twice spent holidays walking from John O'Groats to London. She also travelled widely in France and Germany, and her articles on those travels appeared in the *Glasgow Herald* and *Weekly Scotsman*. She was involved in the amateur drama movement in Edinburgh, appearing in productions and even writing at

least one humorous play. She was also a member of the Dickens Fellowship, and the house she shared with Jessie in Castle Terrace became a
centre of cultural activity. At the same time she was a member of the
Edinburgh Women's Citizens Association. After her death in 1944
(Jessie died in 1937), her 'charm' and 'vivid personality' were extolled.

* * *

Some women doctors were encountered in the last chapter, but in fact
the one most directly involved with the hunger-striking, forcibly-fed
WSPU 'hard core' in the final months leading up to the war was a
member of the WFL whose own activities were very much in line with
that organisation's thinking on civil disobedience. This was Dr Grace
Cadell, who, having been born in 1855, was far from being a young
firebrand when militancy burst onto the scene. She and her sister
Georgina were amongst the first students of Sophia Jex-Blake's
Edinburgh School of Medicine for Women in 1887. As described in
Chapter 2, Sophia's dictatorial manner alienated some of her students,
and Grace and Georgina were expelled for leading a rebellion against
her and were subsequently awarded damages. In the meantime Elsie
Inglis had instigated another medical school for women, so Grace was
able to obtain her degree and go on to practice medicine. She was later
appointed co-equal senior consultant with Elsie Inglis at the Bruntsfield
Hospital.

It does not seem at all surprising that militancy should have
appealed to such a woman, and soon after the WSPU came to
Scotland – in the summer of 1907 – she became president of their
Leith branch. However, when the split came she allied herself with the
democratic Women's Freedom League.

To members of the WFL it seemed quite unjust that a woman, who
was not treated as a full citizen, should nevertheless be subject to taxes
in the same way as a man – 'No taxation without representation.'
Nevertheless, refusing to pay taxes could have serious consequences,
and not many women in Scotland were willing to make such a stand.

Grace Cadell did so. The first time this happened was apparently in October 1912 when the newspapers reported the sale of a chest of drawers owned by her because of her refusal to pay tax. In June 1913 the suffragettes made much more of her principled stance. When her goods were sold at the Mercat Cross, Edinburgh, because of her resisting taxes, there was a 'poster parade' advertising the sale, and a protest meeting was held while the sale was taking place, thereby garnering valuable publicity plus having the opportunity of explaining the logic of such a position to onlookers. Later in 1913 it was reported in *The Scotsman* that Grace Cadell had been prosecuted and fined (without appearing in court) for failing to pay weekly insurance con-tributions in respect of her cook, nurse, house and table maid, and coachman – which is fascinating of itself in showing the extent of her household staff.

From 1913 onwards, when women in Scotland were hunger-striking, and being released and re-arrested under the Cat and Mouse Act (when they could be found), Grace Cadell's home was the first place they were likely to go. When in 1914 the Scottish prison author-ities started forcibly feeding suffragettes in prison, it was again Grace Cadell's house to which they were most likely to head on their release. In May 1914 she described her home to an Edinburgh reporter as 'a house of refuge for the suffragettes'. By July 1914 all suffragette prisoners in Scotland were being sent to Perth prison to be forcibly fed. At the trial of one of them – Maude Edwards, who slashed a picture of King George V in the Royal Scottish Academy – the judge ordered the court to be cleared of suffragettes, and it was reported that many of them resisted the efforts of policemen to eject them, especially Dr Grace Cadell who 'required three officers to remove her'. So she was feisty physically as well as mentally.

Little is known about the last few years of Grace's life. According to her obituary she adopted four children; this must have been during the war years, so perhaps they were refugees. She died in February 1918.

* * *

None of the above women married, but Anna Munro, while dedicating herself to the struggle for the vote, found a sympathetic husband in the course of doing so.

Anna was born in 1883 or 1884, the daughter of a schoolmaster, and grew up in Edinburgh until the death of her mother in 1892, when she and her sister went to live with an aunt and uncle in Dunfermline. She did not need to earn a living, but her conscience led her to social work in the East End of London through the non-conformist Sisterhood of the Poor Movement, which she joined because she admired the organisation's socialist principles. She was an early member of the WSPU, and, in October 1906, back home in Dunfermline, became its branch organiser there. But when the split came in 1907, she followed her friend Teresa Billington-Greig into the Women's Freedom League, becoming her private secretary in 1907. In January 1908 she spent six weeks in Holloway Prison for attempting to take part in a deputation to a cabinet minister. A month later she was appointed organising secretary of the Scottish Council of the WFL, a position she held until 1912.

Anna was responsible for the WFL campaigns on the Clyde coast every summer. Crowds of Glasgow holidaymakers flocked to Dunoon, Largs, and particularly Rothesay on the Isle of Bute, where WFL headquarters were set up, and suffrage speakers found warm and receptive audiences. Educating the public was a key aim of all suffrage societies, and the WFL appear to have been particularly good at this kind of work. In 1911 Anna organised the census resistance in Glasgow. In autumn 1912 she was one of the six women who walked the entire route from Edinburgh to London on the women's march.

After that she campaigned in England rather than Scotland (Hannah Mitchell, an English suffragette, described her as 'a delightful Scottish woman, and an ardent worker'). Tall, elegant, and attractive, Anna was admired by many of the men who heard her speak. She made it a rule not to reply to any letters written by men, but after a meeting near Reading she received a letter from Sidney Ashman, who had been there with his sisters. She thought that 'Sidney' was one of the sisters with whom she had spoken and therefore agreed to meet. He was a member of the Men's League for Women's Suffrage, and Anna married him in April 1913. Shortly after that, Anna was arrested and imprisoned for holding an illegal suffrage meeting in Hyde Park; in 1956 she gave a radio talk entitled 'A Honeymoon in Prison'.

Anna continued to campaign for women's rights and remained active in the WFL until it disbanded in 1961. She also remained active in the Labour Party, serving on local committees, and as both president and chairman of her local party.

Although the couple adopted the surname Munro-Ashman, Anna used only her maiden name for any feminist or socialist campaigning, for fear of jeopardising her husband's road haulage business. The couple had two children. She served as a magistrate for many years, after a leading local landowner correctly predicted that she would be appointed a magistrate only 'over his dead body'. Anna Munro herself died of a heart attack in September 1965.

* * *

The women's suffrage movement seems to have been instrumental in bringing out the full potential of some individuals. This was certainly true of Eunice Murray, the third and youngest daughter of a prominent Glasgow lawyer. She was born in 1877, and spent the rest of her life, in Cardross, Dunbartonshire. Her mother, Frances Stoddard Murray, was born of American parents with strong links to the abolitionist movement, and shared with her husband an interest in all aspects of the women's movement.

In common with a number of the women encountered elsewhere in this book, Eunice was educated at St Leonard's School, St Andrews. Later she became involved in philanthropic activities, being active in the local branch of the League of Pity, volunteering regularly at a local settlement, and advocating temperance. In 1896 she read about the formation of the National Union of Women's Suffrage Societies and commented: 'I should like to join such a society for the question of the emancipation of my sex is a stirring one and leads to vital matters.'

After the militant movement came to Scotland, Eunice Murray, her mother and sister Sylvia joined the WFL. In June 1908 Teresa Billington-Greig asked Eunice to ascertain the views of her neighbours toward women's suffrage. She received such a discouraging response that she concluded: 'If Cardross is an example 'twill be our great great great grandchild that will vote.' But this did not stop her from throwing herself into the campaign, and from 1909 onwards she was the secretary of all 'scattered members' (those who did not live in Edinburgh, Glasgow or Dundee) in Scotland and as such was a member of the executive committee. By 1913 she was president for Scotland of the WFL.

As time went on Eunice found her voice. She was articulate and persuasive both in print and in person, and her letters appeared regularly in the press. She went on to write suffrage pamphlets, including 'The Illogical Sex', 'Prejudices Old and New' and her most popular one, 'Liberal Court' – all published by the Scottish Council of the WFL. In July 1913 the *Glasgow Herald* published a letter from a John Hunter in Rothesay, who had been disappointed when the usual suffrage speaker did not appear, only to be overwhelmed by Eunice Murray: 'Once I heard her convincing, eloquent and logical speech I was quite delighted, and feel persuaded if people had the opportunity of hearing her, and if Cabinet Ministers had that privilege, the vote would be won without delay.'

In 1913 Eunice attended the International Women's Suffrage Alliance conference in Budapest. After her return on 17 November, she was arrested for obstruction after attempting to address a meeting near Downing Street. Although she could not have contemplated taking part in the WSPU's arson and destruction campaign – 'my type of mind could never do the things they do' – she was aware that those tactics brought awareness of the issues to everyone, and she laid no blame on the women: 'No – I blame the Government.'

At the beginning of World War I in August 1914 – before they were called to work in munitions factories and to replace the men swallowed up by the war – many women were thrown out of work, and their plight was a major concern of the WFL. A Women's Suffrage National Aid Corps was formed, with branches in Edinburgh and Glasgow, and Eunice was on the executive committee. The WFL continued to campaign for the vote during the war years. In speeches and articles, Eunice stressed the dangers women would face in the labour market when the fighting ended, and spoke about the changes brought about by the war in the attitudes of women previously in domestic service and other subservient positions. She also wrote a pamphlet, published by the WFL, about all the praise women were getting for their efforts during the war, entitled 'Woman – The New Discovery'.

Eunice had works published in a number of genres, including novels, local histories and a memoir of her mother. In 1930, when most Scottish historians were interested only in political history, she published *Scottish Women of Bygone Days*, in which she broke with the traditional approach and discussed social and domestic life, witchcraft, education, sports, *etc.* The book was dedicated: 'To the women of all ages who defied convention and held aloft the banner of progress.' In 1935 she turned to an older model and produced biographies in *A Gallery of Scottish Women*. An interest in social history developed later in Scotland than in many other countries, but again Eunice Murray was an exception. In *Scottish Homespun*, published in 1947, she wrote: 'Women have a two-fold calling, for not only are we as wives and mothers the guardians of the future, but we are also the custodians of the past.'

In 1918 Eunice was the first woman to stand in a parliamentary election in Scotland – as an independent at Glasgow (Bridgeton) – though she was unsuccessful. In 1923 she was elected onto Dunbartonshire County Council, and the same year became the first president of the local Scottish Women's Rural Institute. But she did not restrict herself to campaigning on local issues and was involved with the National Trust for Scotland from an early stage, serving on its Council and Executive Committee from 1931, and donating to many of its appeals. Eunice Murray was awarded an MBE in 1945 and kept up her connection with the Women's Freedom League until her death in 1960.

Chapter 6
The 'Hard Core'

THIS chapter is about a small group of women who were active and committed to the women's suffrage movement in Scotland until the end. Because their lives during those years were so intertwined, their stories will be told together rather than as individual chronologies.

Janie Allan, born in Glasgow in about 1868, was the only one of them to join the suffrage movement before the arrival of militancy. She was in a unique position, a wealthy woman, daughter of Alexander Allan, owner of the Allan Shipping Line, but belonging to a family of committed socialists. She herself was a member of the Independent Labour Party and was active in social work before becoming involved in the suffrage movement. In May 1902 she was a founder member of the Glasgow and West of Scotland Association for Women's Suffrage. From 1903 she represented the Association on the committee of the National Union of Women's Suffrage Societies.

In December 1906 the WSPU arrived in Scotland, and Janie Allan was immediately drawn to the new style of campaigning. The bulk of the Glasgow Association's members were resistant, but were persuaded to appear at a public meeting at which WSPU officials were to speak, arranged by Janie in March 1907. The rift between the militant and non-militant societies in Glasgow was afterwards too wide for further cooperation, but though Janie subscribed to the WSPU from 1907 she did not resign from the NUWSS committee until February 1909. Even then she remained a member of the Glasgow Association for, as she advised them, though her 'sympathies were more with the militant section of the movement', she knew 'that this Association had done and was still doing good work'. She gave generous sums to the

WSPU and also gave money to the Women's Freedom League until 1912.

The December 1911 *Votes for Women*, the WSPU journal, recorded that Janie Allan had lent her motor car for the North Ayrshire by-election:

> [She] *not only lent us her motor-car, a most valuable asset in a scattered constituency like North Ayrshire, but herself addressed several meetings. She made her debut in militancy at the last protest, and is now beginning her career as a speaker with marked success. Her intimate knowledge of social work among women gave her a special hold over her audiences.*

Also active in that 1911 by-election campaign was Muriel Eleanor Scott though she, and her sister Arabella Charlotte, daughters of an officer in the Indian Army, had earlier belonged to the WFL. Arabella was the older of the two, born in May 1886 in Dunoon. Muriel was born in India, in June 1888. Both women took MA degrees at Edinburgh University and went on to teach. In summer 1908 they were active in the WFL's East Fife campaign and in April 1909 were involved in the WFL's East Edinburgh by-election campaign. In July 1909, under the auspices of the WFL, they attempted to deliver a petition to Downing Street, were charged with obstruction of the police and sentenced to 21 days' imprisonment in Holloway, where they went on hunger strike. At some point between 1909 and 1911 they switched their allegiance from the WFL to the WSPU.

The WSPU organiser for the 1911 North Ayrshire by-election campaign was another university graduate, Frances Mary (known as Fanny) Parker. Born in New Zealand in 1875, she was the niece of the future Lord Kitchener, and her uncle paid for her education at Newnham College, Cambridge, from 1896-98. She went on to teach in France and Auckland before returning to Britain and joining the WSPU in 1908. In February of that year she was sentenced to six weeks' imprisonment in Holloway for taking part in a deputation to the House of Commons. However, she still hoped that the vote would be won by reason rather than by violence, and in summer 1909 she went on a speaking tour throughout south-west Scotland under the auspices of the Scottish University Women's Suffrage Union. And in summer 1910, she spent nearly three months touring Aberdeenshire and Banffshire in Louisa Lumsden's horse-drawn caravan. Fifty-eight meetings were held in 50 different places, again under the auspices of the Scottish University Women's Suffrage Union. In 1911 she was that organisation's delegate to the International Women's Suffrage Alliance congress in Stockholm.

The final woman to consider in this chapter entered the movement later than the others; she was never a speaker or organiser, but such was the strength of her personality and the flamboyance of her actions that by 1914 some newspapers were referring to her as 'the leader of the suffragettes in Scotland'. Ethel Agnes Mary Moorhead was born in the 1870s, one of six children of an Irish army surgeon, and Margaret Humphreys, an Irishwoman of French Huguenot extraction. The family spent time in India, Mauritius and South Africa before returning to Scotland toward the end of the nineteenth century. Ethel's elder sister, Alice, encouraged by their father, qualified as a doctor in 1893 and practised in Dundee. (She married a doctor in Leith in 1908 and died a year later.) For a time in the 1890s Ethel was financially supported by Alice while she studied painting in Paris, but apart from that period she was the stay-at-home daughter who looked after their parents. After her mother died in 1902 there was still her father to care for; he encouraged her painting – she exhibited widely and received praise for her work – and she was devoted to him.

Ethel joined the WSPU in 1910. In December of that year she threw an egg at Winston Churchill at a political meeting in Dundee. In January 1911 she became Dundee's first tax resister. The bailiffs came to the house and removed a candelabrum in lieu, which her friends bought back, to her father's amusement. He died early in 1912 ('the loneliness was terrible,' Ethel commented), and she moved to Edinburgh.

The year 1912 was a turning point for the suffrage movement, for in 1910 and 1911 there was hope that one of the 'Conciliation' Bills might pass and give women the vote, but when Asquith refused to give them any further parliamentary time the 'truce' was over. Janie, Fanny, and Ethel all took part in the three-day London window-smashing raid in March 1912.

It was at the police station after the raid that Ethel first got to know Janie Allan. Ethel wrote:

Her presence had magic and mystery. She was tall, beautiful and very quiet. She used her magic now and persuaded the excited police to send out for tea, bread and butter, scones and jams for the famished raiders.

When Janie was charged in court with damage to the amount of £105, 'she referred to the White Slave Traffic, to the "sweating" of women, to the shamefully small punishments on those who outrage young girls; about these there were no outcries – that was reserved for broken panes of glass'. She was sentenced to four months' imprisonment in Holloway where she distributed comforts to her fellow prisoners. A petition protesting against her imprisonment was signed by 10,500 Glaswegians.

When Emmeline Pankhurst entered Holloway and the WSPU ordered the suffragette prisoners to hunger strike, forcible feeding commenced. Janie barricaded herself in her cell and it took three men, using crowbars, over half an hour to force the door open. She was forcibly fed for a week, and though she did not resist, the effort on her health was 'disastrous – I am a very strong woman and absolutely sound in heart and lungs, but it was not till five months later, that I was able to take any exercise or begin to feel in my usual health again'.

Ethel Moorhead saw Fanny Parker 'pulling stones out of a bag and hurling them at Fuller's Sweet shop'. At the police station, Ethel wrote, Fanny 'was charming with bloom on soft cheeks and cherries in her hat'. Fanny too was sentenced to four months in Holloway and was also forcibly fed.

Amongst Ethel's targets were the windows of Thomas Cook's, the travel agents. But in court the staff of Cook's declared that they had not actually seen her smash them and had only come out when they heard the noise, and another witness gave such muddled evidence that the judge told the jury that there was insufficient evidence to find her guilty; to her astonishment she was released.

Ethel and Fanny smashed more glass in the autumn of 1912. Ethel broke a case at the Wallace Monument near Stirling. The Wallace connection was loaded with symbolism, and at an open-air meeting afterwards Muriel Scott explained that the glass had been smashed 'in order to draw the attention of the people to the fact that their liberty was won by fighting'.

Ethel gave her name as 'Edith Johnston'. She later wrote that this was because her brother in the Indian Army had objected to the family name being dragged through the newspapers, but sheer devilment seems to have been as strong a motive for choosing different names each time she was arrested. She spent a night in Stirling Prison and made a fuss about conditions there after her release. She was then sentenced to seven days at Perth Prison; again, after she left she lodged complaints with the prison commissioners. The governor described her as 'insolent and defiant', and the matron stated that she 'defied all authority and refused to obey any of the Prison Rules'.

Fanny Parker was at this time WSPU organiser in Dundee. One night she and a fellow suffragette smeared some windows with treacle then stuck on brown paper with the words 'Votes for Women' on it, before smashing them. The idea was to deaden the sound, but they were caught and admitted the offence 'as part of a campaign that was being committed throughout the country'. They were sentenced to three days' imprisonment and went on hunger strike, but the short sentence meant that forcible feeding did not have to be considered by the prison authorities. Her uncle, Lord Kitchener, was 'disgusted' when he learned of his niece's involvement in the movement. 'Whatever her feelings on the subject may be,' he wrote to his sister, 'I cannot help thinking she might have some consideration for her family.'

Suffragettes continued to interrupt meetings at which Liberal politicians were the principal speakers, and in Edinburgh in October

1912 at one such meeting nine women arose at intervals to ask about votes for women. All were brutally ejected, and members of the public wrote to Edinburgh newspapers expressing shock at the way the women had been treated. *The Scotsman* claimed that the interrupters had come up specially from London; Muriel Scott retorted that she had been to London only twice in her life, once as a child and again in 1909 'when I experienced His Majesty's hospitality in Holloway'. The others, she insisted, were also Edinburgh residents.

Ethel Moorhead was one of them. She had been hit in the ribs by the man sitting next to her, a maths teacher at Broughton School. About three weeks later she marched into his classroom brandishing a dog whip. He grabbed her and took her to the headmaster's room, where she hit him with her fist. When she was taken into custody she fought against being searched and then broke the window in the cell because 'she thought she had been treated with undue violence'. The court was crowded for her trial, and there was much indignation that she was not allowed to describe the assault on her which provoked her own attack.

In December 1912 Fanny Parker was one of the suffragettes (along with May Grant, who featured in Chapter 4) who was found concealed in the Music Hall, Aberdeen, when Lloyd George, Chancellor of the Exchequer, was scheduled to hold a public meeting there, with the clear intention of causing a disturbance. Ethel Moorhead was outside and threw a stone at the window of a car which she thought contained the Chancellor. When arrested she gave her name as 'Mary Humphreys'. Inside Craiginches Prison she smashed several panes of glass in her windows; the others followed suit and also carried out further protests by refusing to leave the exercise yard and struggling against being carried off. They all went on hunger strike, but the sentence on those who had been inside the hall was only five days, so there was no question of forcibly feeding them. 'Mary Humphreys' was sentenced to ten days, but an unknown sympathiser paid her fine so she was released early.

At the end of January 1913 Asquith, the Prime Minister, addressed a meeting in Leven, and a group of suffragettes tried to get into the hall. One of them, calling herself Margaret Morrison, threw cayenne pepper into the face of a policeman and was arrested. At Methil police station she broke the panes of glass in her cell and then turned the water on in one of the privies, flooding the passage; when the officers finally forced their way in she slung a bucket of water over them. Yes, it was Ethel again – though the authorities did not realise it at the time. From Methil she was removed to Dundee police cells where she again smashed all the panes of glass in her cell. The next day she went on hunger strike.

She scorned the proceedings in Cupar sheriff court. She refused to stand, and when asked if she was in poor health she replied that she was perfectly able to stand. The sheriff said, 'It is very disrespectful to the court', and she responded, 'Yes, I mean it to be'. She denied 'the justice of the proceedings' and therefore refused to plead. She would not lift her veil to allow the police constable to identify her and struggled when another constable tried to lift it, so that the veil was torn and the attempt abandoned. However, Ethel was found guilty and sentenced to 30 days' imprisonment.

Forcible feeding, which was being carried out in England, was discussed within the Scottish prison system, but Ethel struggled so much against an examination by the medical officer that he concluded it would be safer to let her go on starving herself for a few days; in fact she was discharged just two days later.

In March 1913 Janie Allan appeared before the Court of Session for refusing to pay supertax (higher income tax). She pleaded her case in person on the grounds that the statute referred to 'persons': 'If I am not a person for the purposes of the Franchise Acts, I ought not to be considered a person within the meaning of the Finance Acts.' The legal position of a woman, she said, was 'thoroughly illogical and unjust', and she believed that 'it was the duty of every woman to protest against a continuance of this injustice'. Needless to say, she lost her case and had to pay.

In April 1913 the destruction of property by arson, already prevalent in England, reached Scotland. The stand of Ayr racecourse was burnt down in that month, and so was the Perthshire cricket club pavilion. It was either courageous or foolhardy – or both – for Fanny Parker and another suffragette to hold an open-air meeting in Perth the day after that incident. A huge crowd awaited them but gave them no chance to speak, howling them down and pelting them with missiles. The press reported that the women remained cool in the face of very real danger, for even after the police drew batons to protect them the mob pressed on. After such a reception it was not anticipated that suffragettes would again attempt an open-air meeting in Perth, but Fanny Parker was back (this time with May Grant, previously encountered in Chapter 4) in early June and received a much less hostile reception, 'the adult portion of the audience' actually listening to what they had to say, although a younger contingent was abusive. At the end of the meeting the women had to be escorted by the police, who bore the brunt of the missiles thrown at the women.

The successful arsonists were never caught, but four women, and one man, were arrested in connection with an unsuccessful attempt on Kelso racecourse stand. One of them was Arabella Scott. Their trial was held in May, and Arabella was sentenced to nine months' imprisonment, as was the man, Donald MacEwan, although he had only taken the women from Edinburgh to Kelso and played no active part in the attempt. Janie Allan – who was now writing the suffrage column for the socialist journal, *Forward* – bitterly compared his sentence with those imposed on men who had indecently assaulted children, nearly all of whom got considerably less than nine months.

In Calton Jail the prisoners went on hunger strike. The statute popularly known as the Cat and Mouse Act had been passed between the charges being brought and their conviction. Releasing hunger-striking prisoners after only a few days was galling to the prison authorities, but forcible feeding had received such a bad press, with many leading members of the medical profession condemning it, that the government was reluctant to continue resorting to it. The new statute allowed prisons to release hunger strikers when their health was in danger, but under a licence which required them to return on a specified date. The releases and re-imprisonments were to go on until the full sentences had been served. When she was released in late May, Arabella Scott calculated that in order to complete her nine-month sentence, allowing for a five-day hunger strike each time, she would have to go to prison 65 times.

Arabella was interviewed by a reporter from an Edinburgh newspaper after her release, who described her as 'a sweet-faced young lady' though 'obviously weak and ill'. She told him that the prison officers had been kind and humane. Unlike most of the 'mice', who vanished from sight after their first release, Arabella remained at large and was even interviewed by the press after her licence expired on 10 June. She had promised Leith School Board, her employers for the past five years, that she would commit no further acts of militancy, and the Board therefore kept her on its list of teachers. She was re-arrested on 12 June, immediately went on hunger strike, and was released on the 16th. She did not return after her licence expired on the 27th and was briefly lost sight of.

In July 1913 Ethel Moorhead – giving her name again as 'Margaret Morrison' – was caught in a house in Glasgow with fire-lighting equipment, along with Dorothea Chalmers Smith (see Chapter 4). At Duke Street Prison, Ethel smashed the glass in her cell and knocked the prison governor's hat off because he 'dared to stand in the presence of a lady with it on'. When an officer tried to stop her speaking to the suffragettes who presented her with a bouquet of flowers outside the sheriff court, she exclaimed, 'Don't push me. If you put your hands on me again I'll have you in for assault'. The press were rocked by her 'audacity', and it was indeed her total contempt for authority that marked Ethel Moorhead out.

On 24 August Arabella Scott was found taking part in a WSPU protest in London and was re-arrested under the Cat and Mouse Act and returned to Calton Jail. The WSPU had a new policy: in place of a simple hunger strike, suffragette prisoners now went on a hunger and thirst strike, which was far harder to endure and far more damaging to health. Arabella was released on the 29th and went to stay with Ethel Moorhead. But when her licence expired she had once again vanished.

On 15 October Ethel Moorhead and Dorothea Chalmers Smith were tried at the High Court of Justiciary. The women said they intended to defend themselves. When the judge asked them if they would not be better with a lawyer, Ethel replied, 'We usually find they make a muddle of it'. The charge was housebreaking with intent to set fire; as the women had gained access to the house by pretending to be prospective purchasers, the defence was that no 'breaking' had taken place. However, the judge directed the jury that if they thought entry had been secured fraudulently a verdict of Guilty should be returned, and the jury did so. When the judge tried to impress upon the women the gravity of their situation, Ethel interrupted saying that they would not listen to any more and he should just go ahead and sentence them; she was removed for contempt of court. When a sentence of eight months was pronounced the court erupted, with suffragettes bombarding the Bench with missiles.

Naturally the women immediately went on hunger strike. Prisoner 'Morrison' fainted on 19 October but refused to let the doctor examine her. Both women were released on the 20th with the requirement to return on the 27th, but neither did so. Fanny Parker sheltered and hid Ethel. She 'arranged disguises, chose the wigs, – the red one they called Rufus was their favourite and saved their lives as often as it got them into trouble'. Only a favoured few (including Janie Allan) were admitted into the 'mouse hole', and Ethel felt safe with Fanny as 'watchdog'.

Fanny, meanwhile, took part in another incident. At the beginning of November, when a car with Asquith in it was approaching Bannockburn, four women stood in the road and signalled for it to stop. When it showed no signs of doing so, one of the women placed herself in its way, 'deliberately facing the chance of being killed'. The chauffeur managed to stop the car and the women leapt onto the steps and threw cayenne pepper at the occupants. Detectives in a following car seized them and took them to Stirling. It was not in Asquith's interest to prosecute, and the women gave fictitious names, so we might not have known who any of them were, had Ethel not recorded that it was Fanny 'and her volunteers' who 'waylaid and peppered the Prime Minister'.

Fanny, she wrote, 'was an inspiring and daring schemer who always got results .... She was small and looked innocent and disarming with her charming looks, brown eyes, and silky hair. But she had an exquisite *madness*, – daring, joyous, vivid, strategic'.

We have no such flattering description of Ethel at this time. The Criminal Record Office described her as aged 44, 5 feet 6 inches tall, with brown eyes, '(wears *pince-nez*), oblong face, receding chin, slim build, stooping shoulders'.

During the months when Ethel was on the run there were several arson attacks, and the police believed that she was responsible for four of them, three in Perthshire and one in Renfrewshire. In February 1914 she was spotted in Peebles, where she and another woman had been looking round the exterior of Traquair House, and was arrested under the Cat and Mouse Act. She was taken to Calton Jail and immediately went on hunger, thirst and sleep strike. Years later she wrote a vivid description (in the third person) of her state of mind as she paced her cell for hour after hour during the night. Then she was forcibly fed.

When she was told this would happen, 'her rage knew no bounds .... But she had only a toothbrush, and in her hat she found a hat pin'. When the door was about to be opened she pushed the toothbrush underneath and managed to jam it; when a hand tried to push through she jabbed it with her hat pin. But in the end she was overcome and carried to an operating table where she was held down by female wardens while food was poured down a tube by a medical officer from the Morningside Asylum:

The tube from the lunatic asylum was too thick, it filled up all her breathing space, she couldn't breathe .... The young man began pouring in the liquid food. She heard the loud noises she was making of choking and suffocation,

– uncouth noises human beings are not intended to make and which might be made by a vivisected dog .... Still he kept on pouring ....

When she was taken back to her cell all the food came up. In the evening and the next two days the same thing happened. At one point she was convinced that someone had stuck a hot wire in her ear as a form of torture in order to 'break' her.

The directors of the Morningside Asylum were not keen on their staff being employed thus, so another doctor was brought from Peterhead Prison who was experienced at forcible feeding. He was determined to force food down her, but managed to get it into her lungs. She came down with pneumonia. Nevertheless he was determined to continue, and she ended up with double pneumonia. When her story reached the press there were questions in the House of Commons and it was alleged that she brought on the pneumonia herself by tearing her clothes and breaking her cell window. However, Dr Grace Cadell categorically stated that it was food getting into her lungs that had caused the disease. All that mattered to Ethel at this point was being released which, according to her account, came about because of the intervention of a sympathetic Edinburgh lawyer. At first she was not even sure she believed that they would let her go: 'Exquisite sweet-peas sent by Arabella Scott were laid as an olive branch on her bed, – and by this token she knew that what they were saying must be true.'

Scottish suffragettes had not really believed that the Scottish prison system would ever resort to forcible feeding and were appalled when it did so. Dr James Devon, the medical member of the prison commission, told Janie Allan that he 'was of opinion that if a woman's health could only be preserved by allowing her to set fire to other people's houses, we must with regret risk her health'. Various repercussions followed, the most dramatic being the burning down of Whitekirk, one of Scotland's most beautiful medieval churches, within a few hours of Ethel's release. The suffragettes made it very clear that this was a direct response. Reading between the lines of Ethel's memoir, the perpetrator of this deed was Fanny Parker.

Under the Cat and Mouse Act, Ethel was due to return to prison on 9 March. A 24-hour watch was kept on Dr Grace Cadell's house where Ethel was staying, but though a demoralised Ethel panicked at the thought of trying to evade capture, Fanny Parker and Janie Allan were determined. They dressed her in Janie's clothes 'and were particular about the hat which needed careful adjustment with false curls' and managed to smuggle her out. Suspicions were aroused and the police secured a search warrant, but by that time she was gone.

Janie Allan had other concerns as well in March 1914. A public meeting had been arranged in Glasgow at which Emmeline Pankhurst was to speak. Mrs Pankhurst was liable to re-arrest under the Cat and Mouse Act, and she was therefore smuggled into the hall. Trouble was anticipated – indeed, Mrs Pankhurst had written to a friend, 'There is now a Scotch bodyguard and they are eager for the fray'. With a hall filled with 3000-4000 spectators it would have been sensible for the police to behave circumspectly, but instead, as soon as she appeared on the platform they came storming in, and battle was joined. Janie Allan shot blanks from a revolver, and other women flung flowerpots and chairs. The women could not defend Mrs Pankhurst against a large force, but in fact much of the violence took place after she had been captured and dragged off. Members of the audience were horrified at the police behaviour and wrote to the local newspapers to complain.

Janie pressed for a public enquiry. Getting nowhere with the magistrates (who had jurisdiction over the police), she hired a lawyer who recommended that a prominent citizen be asked to act as commissioner for an unofficial enquiry, and that this should be done at once. However, Janie was set on taking part in a WSPU deputation to the King in London, knowing full well that this would lead to arrest and imprisonment. Her counsel wrote to her solicitor that he 'could not imagine anything more foolish or more futile than that Miss Allan should take the step she proposes at the present time'. But Janie was determined and was amongst some 60 women arrested and imprisoned. She clearly felt a great need to share in the suffering being experienced by her friends. The enquiry did not proceed.

At this time, May 1914, Arabella Scott was re-arrested. She had been working as a WSPU organiser in Brighton under an alias; when she was recognised she was returned to Scotland. No one could have described her as a 'sweet-faced young lady' this time, for she resisted every inch of the way, refusing to walk so that she had to be carried, struggling, onto the train. At every possible opportunity during the journey north she shouted out that women were being tortured under the Cat and Mouse Act. On arrival at Waverley Station she again refused to walk and had to be carried, shouting and struggling, to the Calton Jail.

Arabella had gone on hunger and thirst strike the moment she was arrested on 2 May. On the 8th the prison doctor found her in a poor state and she was released that afternoon. However, when taken to Dr Grace Cadell's house she at first refused to leave the vehicle, 'asserting that she would not accept freedom until she was set free uncondi-tionally'. Her sister, Muriel, finally persuaded her. She was due back in prison on the 22nd, but on the 18th a reception was held in her honour and she was accompanied by a large group of suffragettes to Waverley Station where she caught a train to London, thence to Ipswich for a by-election. At Ipswich she and other WSPU members openly defied authority by carrying notices like 'Here is the Mouse, Where is the Cat?'. But, of course, Arabella had given her word to refrain from further unlawful activities, and the authorities felt that arresting her and bringing her back to Scotland was more trouble than it was worth.

Arabella would have been left alone had she not been discovered by accident (on 18 June) in the course of a police raid on a London house in search of another militant. She was re-arrested and again did everything she could to make the journey north as difficult as possible. Naturally she refused to eat or drink, and she would not speak either – until she realised that the train was not stopping at Edinburgh. After Larbert she asked the police officer their destination and was told it was Perth.

The medical officer from Peterhead Prison who had forcibly fed

Ethel Moorhead was now probationary officer at Perth. The prison commissioners had had enough of the Cat and Mouse Act: from this time forward any convicted suffragette in Scotland who went on hunger strike would be forcibly fed at Perth Prison. Arabella Scott was forcibly fed from 20 June until 26 July. During all that time she was completely isolated from the outside world; no letters or visitors were allowed. Her mother wrote to the Scottish Secretary begging for her release: 'She is the daughter of an officer who gave valuable services to the Government of India for twenty-five years on the burning plains of Bengal and I am her widowed mother.' The request was refused, for 'the prisoner has the remedy in her own hands'.

Arabella's own account of her ordeal is harrowing. No less so is the dispassionate daily account by the medical officer of food being poured down her and quantities then being thrown up, and of her volatile mental state during those weeks. He reported that she had not resisted being forcibly fed, though later he admitted that she had 'on two separate occasions which I forgot to record, stated in front of several wardresses & myself that she would shoot me when she got out. Within a few days of her coming here she bit my left forefinger and it became septic'. Arabella emerged from prison feeling more militant than ever.

Another suffragette convicted of attempted fire-raising was also sent to Perth Prison at this time, and the WSPU quickly realised the likelihood that the women were being forcibly fed. The King and Queen were to tour Scotland in July, and Janie Allan used this as leverage when writing to members of the prison commission: the visit would 'present many opportunities for protests of a memorable and disastrous nature, it seems doubly a pity to enter upon a course calculated to entail such serious consequences'. She knew of 'many women, who, 6 months ago, were not prepared to do anything violently militant, but who today would not hesitate'. Protests during the Royal visit would be regrettable, but 'to those who know how high feeling runs against forcible feeding, such incidents would cause no surprise'. The Scottish Office questioned whether proceedings could be taken against Janie in view of her veiled threats, but the Director of Public

Prosecutions advised not. There were various incidents during the Royal visit, but none serious. From 3 July onwards the WSPU staged a constant picket around Perth Prison. Muriel Scott addressed large crowds of over 2000 people, appealing on behalf of her sister and gaining an enormous amount of sympathy.

Meanwhile Fanny Parker was caught trying to burn down the cottage in Alloway where Robert Burns was born. At 2.30 am the night watchman found two women on the premises but was able to grab only one of them. Ethel Moorhead later wrote of Fanny: 'On one dangerous militant duty and adventure when she and her comrade were surprised and about to be arrested she allowed herself to be taken that her comrade might escape.' So the woman who escaped was Ethel.

Fanny gave her name as 'Janet Arthur'. She created a fuss when charged at Ayr sheriff court, denying that the court had any jurisdiction over her, yet while there she also showed her sympathy for a woman who had been sentenced to pay a fine of one pound or undergo ten days' imprisonment for receiving stolen goods, eventually paying her fine. As a prisoner on remand, 'Janet Arthur' immediately put the prison commissioners and Scottish Office in a quandary by going on hunger and thirst strike. The authorities wanted to send her to a nursing home, but she refused to go. They were even willing to allow her to go to Janie Allan's house in Prestwick, except that the police refused the responsibility of keeping a watch over it. So she was sent to Perth Prison to be forcibly fed.

By 14 July, when forcible feeding commenced, she had already been on hunger and thirst strike since the 8th, and she reacted badly to food being poured into her by a tube. It was therefore decided to feed her by the rectum (in spite of the furore when this was done to an earlier suffragette prisoner). 'The manner in which this was done was so unnecessarily painful that I screamed with agony,' she later wrote, and she also mentioned 'a grosser and more indecent outrage, which could have been done for no other purpose that to torture'. A subsequent examination revealed swelling in the genital area and vagina, though this was more likely due to incompetence rather than deliberate cruelty.

Word of her condition reached her influential family, and her brother, Captain Parker, travelled to Scotland and demanded a second medical opinion. On 16 July, when she was released, the Perth Prison medical officer reported that 'her condition is satisfactory', but the outside doctor had a very different opinion, stating that she was 'in a state of pronounced collapse'. She was taken to a nursing home, though the Scottish office was worried that she would escape from there before her trial, making the authorities look even more incompetent. In fact, on 28 July she did precisely that, but as war was declared a week later, and a complete amnesty was announced for all suffragette prisoners, this proved irrelevant.

* * *

As we have seen in earlier chapters, the immediate disbandment of the Women's Social and Political Union and the Pankhursts' jingoistic embracing of the war effort meant that individual members had to choose their own paths. The Women's Freedom League kept its organisation intact, and when at the beginning of the war many women were thrown out of work the WFL started a new London-based department, the 'National Service Organisation', to bring women workers in touch with employers and make sure they were not exploited. The honorary organiser of this new department was Frances M Parker, and her assistant was Ethel Moorhead. Subsequently a branch was formed in Glasgow as well. At this time Janie Allan was on a committee initiated by the Scottish Council for Women's Trades to help women who had lost their jobs.

Later in the war Fanny Parker followed the family's military tradition, being appointed Deputy Controller in the Women's Auxiliary Army Corps (subsequently Queen Mary's Auxiliary Army Corps) in June 1917. She was twice mentioned in dispatches and received the military OBE.

Ethel Moorhead's life continued turbulent. According to an American novelist, Kay Boyle, who met her in France in the 1920s, 'because she painted well and wrote well, she had come over to Paris, in loneliness and discontent with England [*sic*], to settle for a while'. At the Claridge Hotel, Ethel met a striking young American poet, Ernest Walsh. He showed her his poetry, she showed him her paintings, and they started a literary magazine. The first two issues of *This Quarter* appeared in 1925 and contained contributions from Gertrude Stein, Ernest Hemingway, and James Joyce amongst others. The second one contained Ethel's own impressionistic account of her youth and suffrage years, entitled 'Incendiaries (Work in Progress)'.

In 1926 Kay Boyle was taken under their wing. She described Ethel as wearing a simple but expensive plaid

> ... *and she had a Scottish clang to her voice which suited her very well. She had short bobbed hair, with only a little grey in it, and the pince-nez she wore gave her an air of authority; but there was at the same time something like shyness, or wariness, in her small uneasy brown eyes and her tense mouth.*

Kay Boyle stayed at their villa in the south of France and, though a married woman, began a passionate affair with Ernest Walsh. Ernest believed they could live together as a *ménage à trois*, but he died of tuberculosis in October 1926 at the age of 31. Kay Boyle was by then pregnant with his child, and Ethel looked after her. When a girl was born, they falsely declared on the birth certificate that she was Ernest Walsh's legitimate daughter. From Kay Boyle's description the relationship between the two women was a love-hate one. Ethel edited two more issues of *This Quarter* until 1929. In 1934 she edited an edition of Ernest Walsh's poems, and that is the last mention of her name that has been found.

Kay Boyle wrote that all the friends who visited Ethel Moorhead were ex-suffragettes, and Fanny Parker was one of them. She died in early 1924 in the south of France and, by her will, apart from a small bequest to her sister, she left all her property to Ethel Moorhead 'in grateful remembrance for her care and love'. The second issue of *This Quarter* contains a poem and the reproduction of paintings by Frances

Parker. Although Kay Boyle wrote that the journal was funded by Ethel and Ernest Walsh's own money, in 1927 Ethel recorded that it had been founded 'on the strength of a legacy left me by a friend, Frances Mary Parker'.

The executrix of Fanny Parker's will was Janie Allan. Janie lived until 1968 and was a member of the Scottish Council for Women's Trades for many years. She looked forward rather than backward, for in January 1931, when the Suffragette Fellowship asked her for information about her suffrage activities and imprisonment, she replied, 'I don't really think the details you ask for would be of the slightest interest to anyone!'

Arabella Scott followed a more conventional path. She married and emigrated to Australia, where she was an active member of the Australian branch of the Suffragette Fellowship.

Conclusion

THERE were non-militant societies from Ayrshire to Orkney, and 'suffragists' were far more numerous than 'suffragettes', but it was the suffragettes who brought colour and drama to the movement. They grabbed the headlines at the time and have dominated the history of the movement ever since. What is striking, however, is the sheer diversity of women who were active in the suffrage movement in Scotland. Some became involved during Queen Victoria's reign, when the women's sphere was at its most circumscribed. They had to fight on a broad front, not only for the vote, but for further education, a legal existence separate from their husband's, the opportunity to serve on local government bodies, and many other rights that we take completely for granted. Such pioneers had to be strong characters and were not always the easiest people to get along with. Some died before the vote was won, while others were veterans of the Victorian era when the Edwardian campaign burst on the scene. Then there was the new cohort of Edwardian women, politicised and radicalised by the Pankhursts and their Women's Social and Political Union.

What did they have in common? The proportion educated at St Leonard's School in St Andrews is striking. Socialism, or a background in some kind of philanthropic or social work, were important minority strands. They all resented the fact that however well-educated and capable they might be, they were still not considered as equal citizens – an injustice that led to single-issue politics and then, on the part of some, to law-breaking.

After a limited franchise was won in 1918, many of the women continued to campaign on feminist issues, while others turned their interest in politics toward local government, and others followed different paths entirely. For some the suffrage years represented the high point of their lives, while others had such fulfilling later years that the suffrage campaign was only one episode in a rich life.

There were thousands of women involved in the movement in Scotland, only a small number of whose lives are chronicled here. Doubtless there were many who played key roles in the movement and whose lives were every bit as interesting as those related in this account. In some cases it is sheer historical accident that has preserved records which allow the reconstruction of one woman's life and not another's. However, even the most well known of the women here have remained 'hidden from history', so that telling their stories is at least a beginning.

The saddest thing, perhaps, is how few of them remained in Scotland. Many went to England, Australia, or the Continent. Perhaps it was typical of both men and women in that period, that the best and brightest should be attracted to opportunities that seemed to be lacking at home. But it has surely been Scotland's loss.

Index of People's Names

Index of Organisations and Associations